# INDIAN ARCHAEOLOGY TODAY
## *Heras Memorial Lectures, 1960*

CMS

Frontispiece: Painting on pottery of dog or dog like animal
and deer from Nevasa, c. 1100 B.C.

# INDIAN ARCHAEOLOGY TODAY

### H. D. SANKALIA

*Under the auspices of the*
*Heras Institute of Indian History and Culture*

## ASIA PUBLISHING HOUSE
### NEW YORK

The Heras Memorial Lectures honour the memory of an eminent historian and archaeologist, the Rev. Henry Heras, S.J. Father Heras came to India from Spain in 1922 at the young age of 32 to be Professor of Indian History at St. Xavier's College, Bombay. He died there in 1955 after spending more than half of his life in digging up India's past to display to the world the glorious traditions and culture of the land he made his own and whose citizen he became.

Sponsored by the Fr. Heras Memorial Fund and by St. Xavier's College, the Memorial Lectures, which will deal with themes pertaining to Indian History and Culture, were held for the first time in 1960. They were delivered by one of the most distinguished students of the Indian Historical Research Institute which Father Heras founded, and which is now named the Heras Institute of Indian History and Culture. Professor Sankalia, whose fame as an archaeologist is securely established, is at present Joint Director of the Deccan College Postgraduate and Research Institute, Poona.

PRINTED IN INDIA
BY G. G. PATHARE AT THE POPULAR PRESS (BOM.) PRIVATE LTD., BOMBAY 7 AND PUBLISHED BY P. S. JAYASINGHE ASIA PUBLISHING HOUSE, 119 WEST 57TH STREET, NEW YORK

TO
MY WIFE

# CONTENTS

## LIST OF LINE DRAWINGS

## LIST OF PLATES

# LIST OF PLATES

# INDIAN ARCHAEOLOGY TODAY

# I

## CHANGING AIMS AND METHODS
## OF INDIAN ARCHAEOLOGY

### INTRODUCTION

OFFICIALLY, Indian Archaeology is nearly a hundred years old. Next year, 1961, it will celebrate its centenary. Therefore, I welcome this opportunity to review[1] the work in archaeology, specially in the last 20 years, and I am indeed thankful to Reverend Father John Correia-Afonso and Professor William Coelho for asking me to do so. For, I was a student of the Indian Historical Research Institute, which the late Rev. Henry Heras had founded in 1926, and it was here in 1927 that I first heard the name of archaeology. And I believe the Institute which is now called Heras Institute of Indian History and Culture has a claim on me. Whatever position he may occupy in India, a *sisya* always remains a *sisya* to his *guru*. And I consider it a privilege to have to deliver these lectures as a *guru daksina* to the sacred memory of Reverend Father Heras, who if alive, would have simply ordered me to do so. Further, Father Heras always advised us to remain students, and never rest content with the work done in the past. This many of his pupils have done, and I am one of them. So it is in this spirit that I have approached the subject of these lectures.

When the invitation was conveyed to me, it was suggested that the lectures should be useful to the students reading for the graduate and post-graduate courses in Ancient Indian History, Culture and Archaeology, bringing to them new knowledge at present confined to such official publications of excavations called *Reports* and *Bulletins* and that excellent annual account, *Indian Archaeology—A Review,* and *Epigraphia Indica* and *Journal of the Numismatic Society of India.*

[1] For a detailed, exhaustive history of the development of the Department of Archaeology, see the articles by Sourindranath Roy, "Indian Archaeology from Jones to Marshall 1784-1902", and "Fifty Years of the Archaeological Survey of India", by A. Ghosh in *Ancient India,* No. 9, 1953, pp. 4-28; pp. 29-52, respectively.

This suggestion has been kept in mind. At the same time it was thought that this rapid review, while not claiming to be an exhaustive running bibliography, should interpret the new knowledge in a reasonable, understandable form and point out the future lines of work and development of Indian archaeology. Wherever necessary, the information has been documented so as to guide the interested reader. Parts of LECTURE II will be found to be common with those of LECTURES IV and V which I later delivered at the Bombay University. Though not desirable, this step was found to be inevitable, if the new discoveries regarding the "Dark Age" in Indian protohistory were to be properly conveyed to the reader, and their significance assessed.

It would have been impossible for me to refer to all the up-to-date discoveries, had it not been for the kindness of my colleagues working in several parts of India, in the Department of Archaeology, Universities and even in our own Institute at Poona, had they not readily given me information about their work and granted me permission to use it in these lectures. In particular I would mention Shri A. Ghosh, Director-General of Archaeology in India, and the members of his Department, Shri B. B. Lal, Shri M. N. Deshpande, Shri S. R. Rao, Dr. Y. D. Sharma, and Shri B. K. Thapar; then Professor G. R. Sharma, University of Allahabad; Professor B. Subbarao, University of Baroda, and Dr. S. P. Srivastava, Director of Archaeology, Department of Archaeology, Rajasthan, and his colleagues Shri Sagat Singh and Shri Mathur.

BRIEF REVIEW OF AIMS, METHODS AND WORK
(1861-1939)

Though the Department of Archaeology is nearly 100 years old, interest in all old things goes back to the year 1784, when Sir William Jones founded the Asiatic Society in Calcutta with the express purpose of enquiring, among other things "into the History and the Antiquities . . . . of Asia". This was followed by a series of pioneering works by H. T. Colebrooke, Charles Wilkinson, H. H. Wilson, Charles Warre Malet, William Erskine, Salt, Collin Mackenzie and finally Francis Buchanan on epigraphy, the antiquity of Afghanistan, the caves of Ellora, Kanheri and

Elephanta, and the antiquities of Mysore, Bihar and Bengal respectively.

In spite of so much good work, there came an interlude. This was relieved by a short interval when James Princep became the Secretary of the Asiatic Society in 1833 and within three years deciphered the *Brahmi* and *Kharosthi* scripts. Thus were opened the gates of the sources—then known and for nearly a hundred years to come—of ancient Indian history and culture.

However, from 1861 until now, barring a few exceptions, archaeology has remained a Government preserve. Therefore, while reviewing the aims and methods during the past century and the first half of this century, one has perforce to say what actuated the policy of the persons in charge of archaeology.

This long period broadly falls into three divisions as follows: (i) 1861-1902; (ii) 1902-44; and (iii) 1944-60.

Archaeology had a very chequered career in the first period. Twice or thrice the Department (the Archaeological Survey of India, as it was then called), first founded in 1861, was disbanded or severely retrenched. Three personalities—General Alexander Cunningham, James Burgess, and Fergusson—figure prominently during this period in the field of archaeology, as it was then understood, and three or four in that of epigraphy; viz. J. F. Fleet, Bühler, Bhagwanlal Indraji, and E. Hultzsch, names which are familiar to all those who turn the pages of *Epigraphia Indica* and the *Indian Antiquary*.

Cunningham had taken the *Travels of Hiuen Tsiang* (Yuan Chwang) as one of his guides. Hiuen Tsiang was a Buddhist pilgrim who had expressly undertaken an arduous and hazardous journey to India to visit the famous Buddhist places of pilgrimage and other Buddhist centres. Therefore, though a large number of sites in Northern and Central India—in the Punjab, U.P., Rajputana and Central India and the former Central Provinces and parts of Bihar and Bengal—were surveyed on foot, horseback and bullock cart, in days when travelling was much more difficult than today, the one dominant idea that guided this early pioneering work is the discovery of Buddhist monuments.

After Cunningham, the Department was reconstituted, eliminating the co-ordinating authority of the Director-General. Fortunately James Burgess was left in charge of the work in

Western India. Burgess was by profession and aptitude an architect. And all surface monuments, of any architectural importance,
were most carefully drawn, photographed and fully described by
him in several reports. Thus was laid the foundation of monumen-
tal archaeology in Western and Southern India. If we know
anything of the caves and temples of the early dynasties like the
Satavahanas, Chalukyas, Rastrakutas, the Pallavas and the later
Western Chalukyas of Kalyan and Hoysalas, the credit goes to
Burgess and his assistants.

When Burgess left, he recommended a partial dissolution of
the Department that he had built up. Chaos and confusion ruled
the land, from which it was rescued by the vision and foresight,
coupled with strength and vigour, of Lord Curzon. In his minute
of 1900 he defined the aims of the Department which he was
to refound:

> "It is, in my judgment, equally our duty to dig and discover,
> to classify, reproduce and describe, to copy and decipher and
> to cherish and conserve".

This done, John Marshall, who had just completed his training
in Crete, Greece and Turkey, was invited to become the first
Director-General of Archaeology in India. This was a most
happy choice. In him the country found as ardent and forceful
a champion of archaeology as Curzon. His plea for the retention
of the Archaeological Survey, soon after he took charge (1904),
has indeed become memorable and deserves to be engraved in
letters of gold for guidance, whenever, in times of depression or
otherwise, Government wish to abrogate their duty and close
down the Department.

> "I may refer at the outset to an illusory belief to which ex-
> pression has often been given that a time would soon come
> when the Archaeological Survey might be disbanded and the
> work of conservation, if not complete, accomplished through
> the agency of the Public Works Department. That time has
> receded further year after year, and the phantom might now,
> once for all, be laid to rest .... The work of archaeological
> officers is of a kind which cannot be discharged by any other

existing agency and it can only cease if the Government cease to admit their responsibility for the preservation of the ancient remains of the country".

As far as the discovery of the past things was concerned, it received a slightly different direction. Marshall had his training in classical Greek archaeology. Naturally he was interested in discovering Greek elements in Indian culture. However, this was not his sole passion. India was divided into several "circles" and each "circle" was instructed to carry out conservation of typical and important monuments and discovery of new ones. Excavation of a few important sites was also undertaken. The epigraphical branch was also reconstituted. Thus for nearly 30 years—from 1904 to 1934—Marshall guided the policy of the Archaeological Survey of India. Some of the Indian States— like Mysore, Travancore, Jaipur and Baroda—also instituted such Departments following the model set by the Government of India.

The archaeological work during the second period may be grouped into two phases: (i) 1904-1920; and (ii) 1921-1934.

The first phase was interrupted by the war for a few years; but nevertheless, during its short span, scores of inscriptions and religious monuments of several faiths in India were discovered, and a number of sites excavated, principally in Northern India, of which Taxila ranks first and Nalanda second, others in import- ance being Sanchi, Sarnath, Bhita, etc.

These discoveries in the field of epigraphy and monuments have provided the basis for writing several chapters in the political, social, cultural and art history of India, *but not a continuous his- tory of the origin of man and his development through the ages*, or as the anthropologists would put it "the progress of man from Savagery and Barbarism to Civilization". This was due mainly to two reasons. First the aim of archaeology—not only in India, but the world in general—was to find objects which would fill the museum cases, and tell us something about the past. Secondly, it was presumed (though wrongly) that Indian history and cul- ture began with Asoka, and was, thus, not older than the third century before Christ. Naturally all the efforts were concentrated towards unravelling India's past since then. However, the aim was limited; save Taxila which was excavated continuously and extensively for a number of years, no site in India was excavated which tells us of the life of the people at any stage in Indian history. India, dominated by religion, was thought fit to know about its religious monuments only. Thus, it was first the Buddist, then the Brahmanic, Jaina and Islamic monuments which constituted the chief archaeological wealth of the country, and figured prominently in the Archaeological Reports and formed the main content of the syllabi in Universities.

The chance discovery of Mohenjodaro and the re-discovery of Harappa (which was first discovered by Cunningham) to *some extent* helped reshape the policy and aim of the Archaeological Survey. Existence of identical civilizations at a distance of 400 miles naturally led scholars to ponder over the cause of its spread or distribution and origin, though the latter was not investigated at the original type-sites by having deep excavations, right up to the virgin soil. An excellent opportunity was thus lost of knowing the beginnings of civilization in the Indus Valley. But this was compensated for by the knowledge of the civilization itself—a thing which might not have been possible, had the efforts been directed towards its origins. To trace its extent Sir Aurel Stein undertook several exploratory tours in Baluchistan and the Indo —(now Pakistan)—Iranian borderland, and the late N. G. Majumdar explored Sind. These were the first projects which were conceived and undertaken for understanding a particular problem in Indian archaeology. The aim was not to discover *any* ancient object that might be there. It was about this time, 1935, that Cambridge University and the University of Yale co-operated and worked in the Kashmir Valley and the foothills of the Punjab to discover human cultures in association with the Ice Ages.

Man was after all not only 2,300 years old in India. If India boasted of a civilization some 5,000 years ago, then naturally it should have a beginning. The bounds of archaeology in India were thus widening. Poor potsherds and rude stone tools, besides splendid works of art, were beginning to draw the attention of the official archaeologists, though archaeologists in the past century and amateurs in the early thirties had done splendid work in Madras, and the former Baroda State, Kurnool, Bombay and the Punjab.

The official outlook, however, still remained comparatively closed. All the Europeans—mostly British officers—had left, and Rao Bahadur K. N. Dikshit was in charge of the Archaeological Survey as the Director-General of Archaeology in India. It was then suddenly realized that the Archaeological Department —one of the largest in the world—had not done so well in its life of 30 years, in the matter of conservation as well as excavation. Sir Leonard Woolley, the famous excavator of the Royal Graves of Ur and many other sites in Western Asia, was invited to suggest remedies for improvement. Then came the war.

## NEW AIMS AND METHODS

Archaeological work, particularly excavation, was much restricted, because of the strong adverse comments of Sir Leonard Woolley. Only the Director-General, according to him, was competent to carry out a scientific excavation, and he recommended that attention be now turned to Ahichchhatra, a site in the Gangetic Valley, for knowing the evolution of Indian Culture.

It was at this time that the Deccan College had been re-opened as an Institute for post-graduate studies and research in History and Linguistics. A professor there had submitted to Rao Bahadur Dikshit certain schemes for exploration. While working with very limited means, and in a very narrow geographical sphere, viz. Poona District, certain megalithic monuments were discovered near Poona. These had been completely neglected, because they were architecturally of no use, much less beautiful. But it was forgotten or not realised that these rude stone monuments enshrined a particular stage in man's cultural development. For it was the aim of the Department, called the Proto-Indian and Ancient Indian History Department, to search for links between ancient Indian history and proto-Indian history on the one hand and between proto-Indian and prehistory on the other, so that a continuous history of man's past in India can be had.

Rao Bahadur Dikshit was not slow to realize the importance of this discovery. It was not indeed very significant, but it led to what is now called a "chain reaction", and was responsible for determining the future lines of work in the Deccan College and in India.

## CO-OPERATION BETWEEN GOVERNMENT AND RESEARCH
### INSTITUTIONS

Rao Bahadur Dikshit and I had independently suggested that the problem posed by Robert Bruce Foote of a hiatus between the Palaeolithic and Neolithic Ages, after his pioneering work in Gujarat in the last century, be taken up for investigation. This he now asked the Deccan College and the Gujarat Research Society to undertake with the help and co-operation of the Government of India. This was a landmark in the development of Indian archaeology in two ways. For the first time explorations, followed by small excavations, were to be undertaken with the sole aim of attempting to solve a problem. It was indeed a very important problem. What had happened to man in Gujarat some 2,00,000 years ago? Did he leave the region all of a sudden without leaving any traces owing to certain climatic reasons, or did he gradually step into a food-producing stage, known as Neolithic?

Secondly, it was the first time that the Government of India had come down from its ivory tower and sponsored archaeological work in co-operation with a private society and a provincial Research Institute. About the same year the University of Calcutta was granted a licence to excavate at Bangarh in Bengal. This was a very small beginning and was symbolic of the change —a revolution—that was to follow very soon, both in the outlook —the aim and objectives of archaeological work in India—and the agencies that were to carry it out.

But, perhaps, after an existence of nearly 40 years, this was probably a very slow, halting step. Some dynamic action was necessary to remould archaeology in India. This was achieved by Dr. (now Sir) Mortimer Wheeler. Wheeler was endowed with a unique combination of theoretical and practical training, varied experience of archaeological work, military discipline and an innate sense of planning. Within a couple of months of his arrival he realized that Indian archaeology had suffered from a lop-sided development. A few Buddhist sites in Northern India had received all the attention, the South was completely neglected (because of its hot climate!). Nor was there any fixed point in its chronology before the 4th-5th century A.D., because there were no dated inscriptions or any other reliable source of information by which one could understand the sequence of events backward in South Indian history.

However, the first essential was a trained body of workers. So far archaeological excavation was a closed book to students in Indian Universities. Wheeler opened this. Actually he wrote to the Vice-Chancellors of various Universities to depute students for training in the excavations camp at Taxila, Arikamedu and Brahmagiri. And just to encourage them, and help them while they were receiving training there, he paid them their living expenses or small stipends.[2] Happily this practice is continued by Sir Mortimer's successors, and by institutions which conduct excavations.

## "TIME-TABLE" OF CULTURES

Why did Wheeler insist on a "time-table", as he so aptly and beautifully called the pressing need in archaeology? Why was it not thought of before?

The reason is very simple. Formerly the aim of the archaeologist was to get any old, ancient, artistic object which would satisfy the curiosity of the layman, and the connoisseur of art. None of them cared a bit about how man and his culture had evolved. But if you want to trace the development or evolution of any thing, whether it be a man, or a flower or a tree, or a work produced by man, you must see the various steps which had to be crossed to reach a particular stage. To take a concrete instance, in South Indian history (because we had already a hazy notion of things in North India about Asoka, Chandragupta, Buddha, etc.) when was it that the people erected huge megalithic tombs of which South India had hundreds? Were they prehistoric, as it was universally believed before Wheeler, or later? These should be so excavated that they provided a link with something known. Wheeler was conversant with Roman antiquities and so he set about looking for these, if they were there. In a visit to Pondicherry he saw Roman *amphorae* and Arretine pottery, so

---

[2] Both these practices were advocated by the writer when he returned from England after having had training under Dr. Wheeler in an article which the *Illustrated Weekly of India* called "Archaelogy for the Masses," March 1938.

he dug at Arikamedu.[3] This provided a fixed datum line for knowing what things India made and what she imported in the first century B.C.—A.D. The next step was taken at Brahmagiri and Chandravalli, where objects contemporary to and earlier and later than those found at Arikamedu were found. A rough time-table of cultures was ready for the Southern, Western and South-eastern India. It was based on the principle "proceed from known to unknown".

### IMPORTANCE OF POTTERY

Pottery which is rarely found in complete form, played an important part in building up this sequence of cultures. It had been completely neglected earlier. Slightly noticed in the extensive work at Taxila, it had received full attention at Mohenjodaro and Harappa. This led to pottery-hunting of similar type, fabric and design by Aurel Stein and Majumdar in Baluchistan and Sind respectively. However, pottery of the historical period had not found a place in archaeological reports, save very perfunctorily. By the discovery and recognition of the Northern Black Polished Pottery (NBP), then the imported Mediterranean Arretine ware and the *amphorae*, and the association of a fine black-topped and red-bottomed pottery called the Black-and-Red Ware, and a pottery with a glossy yellowish-reddish tinge with criss-cross painting on it, a *corpus* of Indian pottery forms and fabrics began to be built up.

What were coins and inscriptions to the earlier archaeologists, pottery and palaeoliths are to their present day successors. Both the latter are more trustworthy as indicative of past cultures than coins and inscriptions, for the coins can migrate very easily, whereas the inscriptions may relate only to the written form of letters, and the donor, his family, etc. But pottery belongs to the place and the people or is definitely imported. Once baked in fire, it is almost imperishable and studied intelligently will reveal an important aspect of the life of the people who made it.

So for detecting past buried cultures and their sites, there is nothing so valuable as pottery.

[3] This has been vividly described by him in *Rome Beyond the Imperial Frontiers*, London, 1954, p. v. (preface).

After recognizing a pottery form and fabric, even from its fragments, called "potsherd", as characteristic of a particular period and region, the archaeologist goes about looking for similar forms and fabrics. This is called "exploration".

## DISTRIBUTION MAPS

The sites which yield similar type are plotted on a map (Fig. 1). These maps tell us about the range of the culture, as indicated by a particular type of pottery. Thus the NBP is primarily confined to the Gangetic Valley, having come into existence about the 6th-5th century B.C. Buddhist *Bhiksus* took it to far off places during their preregrinations, and so occasionally sherds are found as far south-west as in Nevasa, Nasik and Kolhapur; or south as in Amaravati on the Krishna; west as far as Somnath; east as far as Gaur and Pandua in East Bengal; in north in Taxila and Charsada, and as far as Udigram in the Swat Valley in Afghanistan.

Distribution maps have thus come into vogue. These can be for anything, not necessarily pottery. A look at the distribution map not only reveals the extent of a particular artifact, but makes us think if the objects are from far too distant regions, such as India and Europe, or India, Egypt and South-East Asia; and urges us to seek for an explanation of identical forms in such far-flung places and for the agencies which contributed in their transmission.

## PALAEOLITHS

Above a reference was also made to palaeoliths. *"Palaeo"* means "old", and *"lithos"* stands for "stone" i.e. an "old stone" and connotes in archaeology an Early or Old Stone Age tool, made by man thousands of years ago. Our experience tells us that such tools are not made today (except in France where such things are in great demand by wealthy tourists and a business in faked tools has grown up). Further, when they are found in a particular geological context, the tools indicate their age in a fairly certain manner. So after our work in Gujarat in 1941-42 in the valleys of the Sabarmati, Orsang and others, similar search was started in the Godavari and its tributaries in Maharashtra. But to our surprise the tools found were of a different nature and rock, the significance of which could not be immediately understood. Then once again such tools were found at Nevasa, Ahmadnagar District, in 1954 in the bed of the Pravara, along with much older types of tools of an earlier age. So it dawned upon us that these new types of tools belonged to another—a later—Stone Age. And since then such tools are being reported by explorers from several parts of India. The distribution maps reveal that this Stone Age was almost co-extensive geographically with that of the first. Further studies might bring to light its relation with similar Stone Age Culture in Africa.

Thus the past decade or generation may rightly be called "the Age of Pottery and Palaeoliths".

These distribution maps when related to geography further give us an insight into the environment in which man lived or alternatively to the physical barriers which an emergent culture, that is the people bearing it, had to face, or the factors which facilitated its spread.

### STRATIGRAPHICAL METHOD OF DIGGING

With the reorientation in our aims and objects, the means for realizing these have necessarily changed. I have mentioned some of the newer techniques. These were already known and practised in Europe, at least a generation earlier, but as the anthropologists say, for introducing them into India, new cultural or other forces were necessary. However, the West had in the meantime still marched ahead. Archaeologists and geologists have been trying to discover better and more exact means of dating the past. So, when the archaeologists working in Western Asia were relying on written evidence like coins, seals and inscriptions, or various building levels, or failing both these, on stylistic evidence, Wheeler introduced the stratigraphic method in our excavations, and the three dimensional system of recording the finds.[4] In other words, it is nothing but the principle of superposition of layers which are to be carefully observed and recorded while conducting an excavation. It is an extension of the geological method into archaeology. When the objects are not only noted according to their

---

[4] See *Ancient India*, No. 3, 1947, pp. 43-50 and Wheeler, Sir Mortimer, *Archaeology from the Earth*, Oxford, 1954.

depth, but their exact position in space is further recorded by noting their position from a fixed point, it is possible to prepare an exact plan of where the objects were when they were excavated (Figures 2, and 2b).

Though comparatively more exact, the stratigraphic method is certainly very expensive and time consuming, and at best indicates a relative sequence of events. Wheeler himself has suggested certain modifications [5] in its application in a country like India and on a site like Mohenjodaro, in a brilliant lecture entitled "What Matters in Archaeology?".

So the search for more exacting method for dating the past was on. For, every one is curious to know the antiquity of an object he has found, whether he is a scientist or a layman. It is a common human instinct. While the geologists, astronomers and others were playing with various methods since the last century, an admirable account of which you will find in Professor Zeuner's *Dating the Past*,[6] the physicists developed a more exact method. It is indeed an offshoot of the atomic explosion studies which has developed since the conclusion of the last war, and is due to

[5] After fully condemning the methods adopted by the excavators of Mohenjodaro, Wheeler makes a very pertinent remark. He says that, granted their methods were bad and unscientific, without a large-scale excavation of that nature, the great Indus Civilization—with its houses and well-aligned streets—would never have been laid bare before the world. While archaeologists like himself, following the stratigraphical method of excavation first introduced by General Pitt-Rivers in England as far back as 1880, would have at best given an idea of the evolution of cultures at Mohenjodaro by relating the various pottery types and seals, for instance, to a careful observation of the layers, they would have produced an adequately documented Indus Valley Culture, but missed the Indus Civilization. And what after all *matters* to archaeologists as well as to layman alike is an insight into the life of the past, its *complete re-creation*, as far as possible, before our eyes. It is therefore necessary, as Sir Mortimer says, to have something like selective stratification on great sites like Mohenjodaro, and not a slavish imitation of Pitt-Rivers, which the latter himself would have adopted. It is all right for small sites which hardly yield 10 potsherds in an entire excavation.

The entire lecture is worth reading. See Wheeler, R.E.M., "What Matters in Archaeology?", *Antiquity*, Vol. XXIV, 1950, pp. 122-30.

[6] Several editions of this most useful work have since been published since its first appearance in 1946.

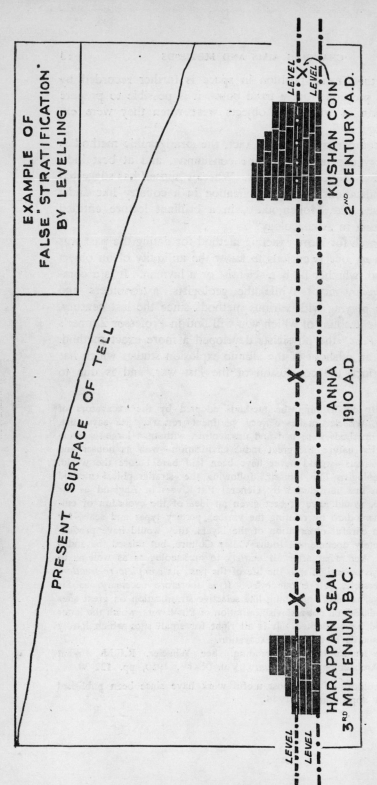

EXAMPLE OF
FALSE "STRATIFICATION"
BY LEVELLING

PRESENT SURFACE OF TELL

LEVEL
LEVEL
X
KUSHAN COIN
2ND CENTURY A.D.

X
ANNA
1910 A.D

X
HARAPPAN SEAL
3RD MILLENIUM B.C.

LEVEL
LEVEL

Figure 2(a)

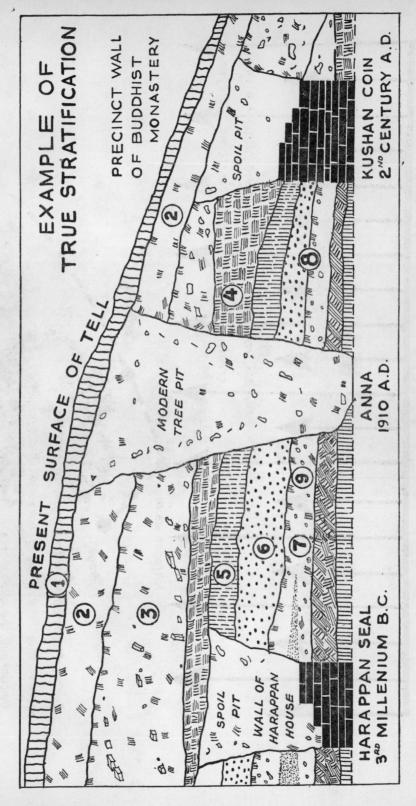

EXAMPLE OF TRUE STRATIFICATION

PRESENT SURFACE OF TELL

PRECINCT WALL OF BUDDHIST MONASTERY

SPOIL PIT

MODERN TREE PIT

SPOIL PIT

WALL OF HARAPPAN HOUSE

KUSHAN COIN 2ND CENTURY A.D.

ANNA 1910 A.D.

HARAPPAN SEAL 3RD MILLENIUM B.C.

Figure 2(b)

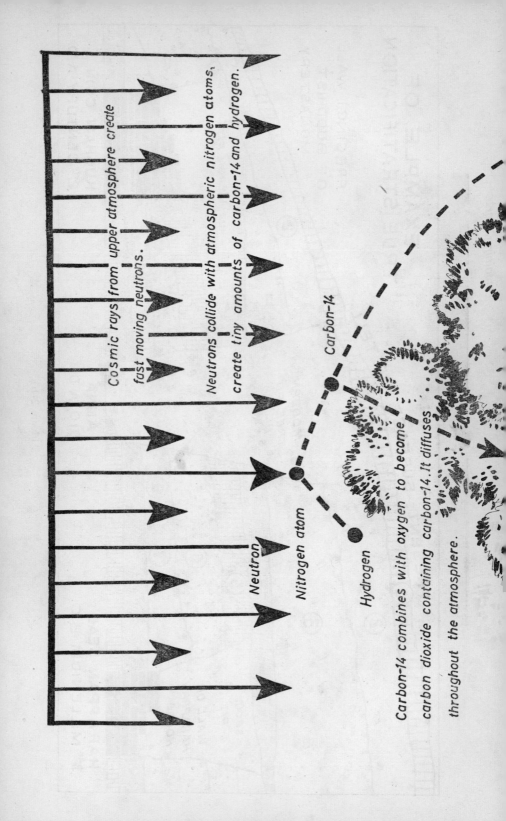

Cosmic rays from upper atmosphere create fast moving neutrons.

Neutrons collide with atmospheric nitrogen atoms, create tiny amounts of carbon-14 and hydrogen.

Neutron

Nitrogen atom

Hydrogen

Carbon-14

Carbon-14 combines with oxygen to become carbon dioxide containing carbon-14. It diffuses throughout the atmosphere.

Willard F. Libby, working as nuclear chemist at the University of Chicago's Institute for Nuclear Studies.

## CARBON-14 OR C-14 METHOD OF DATING

The carbon-14 method, very briefly and in simple words[7], is based on the discovery that vegetation—trees, plants, flowers—absorbs, carbon dioxide, which contains carbon-14. Our atmosphere is full of this and the process goes on every minute. The cosmic rays bombard the upper atmosphere. This produces, fast-moving neutrons. Neutrons collide with atmospheric nitrogen atoms, producing tiny amounts of carbon-14 and hydrogen. Finally carbon-14 combines with oxygen to become carbon-dioxide.

When animals feed on vegetation they add carbon-14 to their bodies. But when plants and animals die, carbon-14 disintegrates and reverts slowly to nitrogen. (Fig. 3)

It is indeed remarkable and useful to archaeology that all living organisms contain the same proportion[8] of carbon-14. And after

[7] Adapted from *National Geographic Magazine*, August 1958, pp. 234-55. The article "How Old is It" is very instructive.

[8] This assumption has recently been questioned in "The 1959 Carbon-14 Symposium at Gröningen". Of this Professor H. T. Waterbolk has given a very useful summary in *Antiquity*, XXXIV, 1960, pp. 14-18, from which the relevant extracts are quoted:

Of great importance were discussions on the validity of the assumption that the radioactivity of living matter has always been constant. In *Antiquity*, XXXII, pp. 161-2, Mr. Barker has explained the 'Suess effect', the lowering of radioactivity in consequence of the modern combustion of coal and oil. He also referred to recent investigations by De Vries showing that even before the Industrial Revolution, the level of radioactivity had fluctuated. This had been discovered through the high-precision measurement of tree-rings of known age. Cambridge, Copenhagen and Heidelberg have collaborated on this problem and they would now confirm De Vries's results for a much longer period (the last 1200 years). It was agreed that the mean value established for the radioactivity of living matter should be chosen as a basis for future age calculations. This level of radioactivity appears to be about 95 per cent of the activity of oxalic acid from the National Bureau of Standards in Washington. This material, sufficient amounts of which are available, will henceforth be the international gauge sample and 95 per cent of its activity will be the 'recent standard'. (*Contd. on p. 18*)

death organic materials lose their carbon-14 at the same rate. It is calculated that half disappears in 5,568 years, a half life. Three-fourths dissipates in two half lives, and so on. When, therefore, the radioactivity of modern carbon is compared with radioactivity in ancient carbon, either from charred grains, wood, bone or shells, it tells us the amount of time that has elapsed since death (of the sample examined). It has thus become possible to calculate in almost exact years the date of the site, or building, which yielded the sample. The earliest date—58000 B.C.—so far is of a piece of wood unearthed at Amersfoort in the Netherlands which, however, does not prove the existence of man. Earlier C-14 dates for the existence of man, viz., 35000 B.C. and 32000 B.C. respectively, have been given by charcoal from Texas, North America and the Shanidar Cave in Iraq. The first agricultural

> Two consequences are of great importance to archaeologists. In the first place, all dates published upto now will have to be recalculated to the new standard. For the greater number of laboratories, the changes will be much less than the statistical error, and therefore not of much significance. For a few laboratories, however, the number of years to be added is considerable. For Gröningen it will be about 200 years. Exact figures cannot yet be given, since they depend on, among other things, planned remeasurements of the C12-C13 ratio in the N.B.S. oxalic acid. The changes will be published in one of the next volumes of the *American Journal of Science, Radiocarbon Supplement*. In this periodical, one issue of which has already appeared, future date lists will be published.
>
> Of more importance, however, is the fact that, after applying the above-mentioned correction, we shall have to take into consideration the fluctuations in the original level of radioactivity in living matter. This value has been found to be equivalent to, at most, some 160 years; it may be either below or above the mean value. This means that an extra uncertainty is added to the statistical error. Whatever high degree of precision may be obtained by the physicist in the actual measurement, the profit for the archaeologists will be limited by this systematic error.
>
> On the one hand this is definitely a disappointing result, especially for those who had very high hopes for precision dating by carbon-14. But on the other hand, it is good to have been told exactly where we stand on these matters, and we ought to be extremely grateful to the physicists who have taken so much trouble with the difficult time-consuming measurements. There are still a vast number of Early Neolithic, Mesolithic, and Palaeolithic problems for the solving of which the radio-carbon method will be of immense help.

village of Jarmo in north Iraq goes back to 7000 B.C., though earlier still is Jericho in Palestine. In India, so far, we have got four C-14 dates for the Chalcolithic village of Navdatoli on the Narmada in Central India, ranging between 1700 B.C.—1100 B.C., for the sites of Utnoor and Pikhlial in Andhra Pradesh, and for Kot Diji, an early Harappan site in the former Bhawalpur State in Pakistan. The last date shows that the typological dating of the Indus Civilization to about 2500 B.C. was right.

## ARCHAEO-MAGNETISM

Other methods are also being tried. One of these is called "archaeo-magnetism or remnant magnetism".[9] It is based on the principle that many rocks—that is, stones and natural clays—contain oxides of iron and are feebly but appreciably magnetic. And it has been found that remains of ancient kilns, hearths and burnt structures do preserve their magnetization. This can be measured and compared with the direction of the earth's field at present. In this way a graph might be prepared for nearly 2,000 years, and thus date a particular object within a quarter of a century.[10]

## THERMOLUMINISCENCE

Two new archaeological dating methods [11] now enable scientists to date objects 60,000 years farther back in time than they have been able to do before.[11a]

One records the electron glow of dishes, vases and other pottery when heated; the other measures moisture layers in objects made of volcanic glass.

All materials contain traces of radioactive elements, which emit radiation that traps electrons in solid crystals at ordinary temperatures. As this process progresses, the number of trapped electrons increases.

Doctors George C. Kennedy and Leon Knopoff of the University

---

[9] R. M. Cook and J. C. Belshé, "Archaeomagnetism: A Preliminary Report on Britain", *Antiquity,* Vol. XXXII, 1958, pp. 167-78.
[10] This method is still at an experimental stage.
[11] *Science Digest,* Aug. 1960, p. 35. [11a] For another method *see* p. 24.

of California Institute of Geophysics, Los Angeles heated pottery and lava rock to about 800°F. At this point trapped electrons are released and they create a glow called thermoluminiscence.

This glow is so faint that it is not visible, but it can be detected and measured by a photomultiplier tube. The more light emitted, the greater the length of time since the material was last heated to a temperature where it could give off electrons. In the case of a piece of pottery this would probably be when first fired or when last used in a hot fire.

The thermoluminiscence technique can date objects up to about 100,000 years old. It has been used to date 15,000-year-old lava rock from Arizona and ancient Greek pottery from the ninth century B.C. or about the time when Homer was writing the *Iliad*.

This dating method will be especially valuable in establishing dates and time sequences for prehistoric societies that have left no materials containing carbon, such as charcoal or wood, which can be dated by the radioactive carbon method.

It will also help to establish the correct chronology of varying styles and shapes of pottery. Archaeologists most commonly use a comparative dating method by considering such things as development of craftsmanship, decoration and design. The thermoluminiscence technique can now be used to verify or correct the archaeologist's chronology. It is expected to be used next in dating Mayan and Mexican pottery. This method will have great scope in India where several regional and sub-regional cultures based solely on pottery have recently been unearthed, but their exact age is not known.

### AERIAL PHOTOGRAPHY

Methods of detecting the site hidden from view have also been developed. Aerial photography has been practised since the first world war in England, Europe and Western Asia. In India aerial photographs are taken of sites already known, but the method has not been used for discovering new sites, except at Charsada in Pakistan. But the classic example of the usefulness of this device is the discovery of hundreds of Etruscan tombs in Italy. By studying shadings of the soil, relative growth, vegetation shadows and markings revealed in the oblique light of dawn or sunset, and with the help of new films and filters and three dimensional viewers aerial pictures can almost be said to "talk". And Banditaccia (north of Rome), a city of tombs with its outlines of vanished roads, or buried ruins invisible from the ground showed as on an X-ray.

## ELECTRICAL RESISTING SURVEYING

Even when aerial photographs have indicated the existence of ancient sites, "the markings they show must be found on the ground". This is often difficult, and at times impossible, because "they may have been blotted out entirely by farmer's ploughs". However, with this method, it is possible to detect irregularities or buried features, to "see" into the ground. Hidden rocks, walls, terraces, roads or tombs may be found and pin-pointed. This is done by sending an electric current along a predetermined path and by measuring differences in electrical potential at given points.

## MAGNETIC PROSPECTING OR SURVEYING

To this has now been added magnetic prospecting[12] or surveying. It is "complementary to aerial photographing in that it gives exact location on the ground and that it responds well to isolated features such as pits and kilns. Though it is not sensitive to stone walls and foundations, it is particularly sensitive where fire or food is concerned." In England, recently, "using two proton magnetometers, each with a team of three operators, a basic survey of the whole of four areas was completed in eight hours". Where the occupation debris are not thick, but comparatively thin, say about 24 inches—which is very rare in India—this method will prove extremely expeditious in detecting ancient finds.

## PHOTOGRAPHING THE INTERIOR OF A CAVE WITHOUT EXCAVATION

The most wonderful thing is that the Etruscan tombs, ranging

[12] *Antiquity,* Vol. XXXIII, 1959, pp. 205-07.

in date between the 8th and the 2nd century B.C., but a great
number of about the 6th century B.C., are now being photographed
from inside without excavation with the help of a periscope
camera. It includes a photographic drill consisting of a three
inch tube which is fitted with a tiny Minox camera. This takes
a film only slightly larger than that of a 8 mm. home movie. A
high-intensity photoflash unit behind another window in the tube
provides light. The tube is lowered through soil, rock and the
roof of the tomb itself, in a hole previously bored by an electric
earth drill. Remote control then triggers the light and camera,
advancing the film after each exposure. In 12 shots, turning the
tube 30 degrees after each one, the entire interior of the tomb is
thus photographed.

With this "Eye of Minos" as the contraption is dubbed, it is
possible not only to tell if a tomb is empty or hopelessly disinte-
grated, forestalling useless excavation, but also to make an exact
photographic record of the contents of a sealed chamber before
it is opened to the light of modern day.[13]

We have thus travelled a long way in the last 100 years. No
longer is the aim of archaeology "to have an accurate description
—illustrated by plans, measurements, drawings, or photographs
and by copies of inscriptions—of such remains as deserve notice"
or "a complete search over the whole country and a systematic
record and description of all architectural and other remains that
are remarkable for their antiquity or their beauty or their historical interest", as was defined by Cunningham in 1870, according
to the needs of the times; or a history of art as envisaged by
Burgess in 1886; or, as Lord Curzon so nobly put it in 1902, "it
it our duty to dig and discover, to classify, reproduce and describe, to copy and decipher and to cherish and conserve".

Nor is it sufficient to have a knowledge of mere "chronological
sequence", as Sir Leonard Woolley recommended, or a time-
table of sequence of cultures, as Dr. (now Sir) Mortimer Wheeler,
so tellingly expressed in listing the needs of Indian Archaeology
in 1944. Each of these aimes or objectives might have been justified by the circumstances prevailing at each period when these

[13] Adapted with slight omissions from an article by Carlo M. Lerici,
"Periscope on the Etruscan Past", *National Geographic Magazine,* Vol.
CXVI, No. 3, September 1959, pp. 336-50.

aims were laid down. (And I for one would not criticize our predecessors, for we are all creatures of time and circumstances, and become wiser after the event.)

### KNOWLEDGE OF THE "WHOLE MAN"

The aim now is—whether it be in India, England or America— to know the whole man: the objects, artistic or otherwise, made by him and the environment in which he lived, viz., the climate, the flora and fauna, and man's social, religious and economic status, including even the probable guess as to the density of population, and finally the stage or stages by which he reached the particular stage under study.

### EXCAVATION AND CRIME DETECTION

Consequently the excavation, and the preceding and consequent exploration, has become something like the work of Sherlock Holmes, where nothing is neglected, much less discarded. Most minute changes in the colour of the soil or earth excavated are recorded, collected and scientifically examined, and the same care is bestowed on the ash or charcoal as on a precious object of art. If it is an architectural monument, not only is it carefully drawn and photographed, but all possible means are employed to learn about its significance—about the nature of the stone used and its source, about the technique of manufacture—so that we may learn not only about its architectural style, but also about the social, economic, industrial and religious milieu which were responsible for its creation.

Nor is all this attention to be devoted only to one particular period of history or prehistory of this country or that. The same care, the same attention, is to be shown to everything, everywhere. For archaeology has become universal in its appeal.[14]

The aim of archaeology being so all-embracing—touching every

14 In corroboration of this may be cited the recent symposium on "From 15,000 B.C. to the Thresholds of Urban Civilization—A World-wide Consideration of the Cultural Alternatives," held by the Wenner-Gren Foundation for Anthropological Research at Burg Wartenstein near Vienna.

aspect of human life and its relation to animal, vegetation and physical world around man—the methods of achieving these aims are being constantly refined. Thus by broadening our aims and our perspectives and by perfecting or modifying our methods[14a] the entire humanity's past will be recreated.[15]

[14a] According to a new method called "Pottasium Argon" which was tried on the skull and jaw found at Olduvai, Tanganyika, East Africa, man and the associated tools are 1,750,000 years old.

[15] After writing this I came across Professor Grahame Clark's Presidential Address, "Perspectives in Prehistory" to the Prehistoric Society, London, in 1959 (*Proceedings of the Prehistoric Society for 1959*, New Series, Vol. XXV, pp. 12-14), wherein he says:

Whatever our interests, whatever special area or period we may prefer to study in detail, our work is likely to be better as well as more worthwhile if we view our immediate task in the broadest perspective, as part of an effort to understand the common past of humanity. I have just said that from some points of view their histories are among the most important products of the great literate traditions of humanity. I believe that a comprehension of prehistory will prove to have been one of the most significant achievements, and requisites, of the world-wide society which is even now struggling for the first time into existence. By and large the history of history is the history of expanding conceptions of what constitutes history. The scope of history has grown with the scope of social awareness, from the history of the hunting band to that of the village, from the history of oral traditions to that of the written record, from the history of nation or civilization to the history of mankind. To-day we are being knit together, not merely by improving means of communication and by the material nexus of industrial civilization, but increasingly by an awareness of our common heritage as men: it is by enhancing and deepening this awareness that societies like our own have most to contribute, and the quality of their contributions will depend more than anything else on the perspective from which they view history.

# II

# INDIAN ARCHAEOLOGY AND ITS CONTRIBUTION TO PREHISTORY AND PROTOHISTORY

In the first lecture I have described to you how the aims and perspectives of archaeology were being widened not only in India, but all over the world, and how and what new methods were being employed in attaining these aims. And it may well be asked "how have these changing aims and methods contributed to our knowledge of the various periods in which man's history is conventionally divided into prehistory, protohistory and ancient history?" Our attention will be primarily focussed on India, though important discoveries made elsewhere will be referred to if and when necessary.

Before entering into details, let us understand what is meant by 'prehistory' and 'protohistory': how are these distinguished or differentiated from each other on the one hand and from history on the other.

The definition of 'history' is too well known. Briefly it is a written account of an incident, place or country, a person or a nation. If written by an eye-witness or immediately after the happening of the event, it is called 'contemporary history'; but, whenever recorded, the essential feature is that it is recorded in writing.

## PREHISTORY

Now it is this feature which distinguishes history from prehistory; the latter, prehistory, deals with a period when writing was unknown in or to the particular country or amongst the people whom we are studying, and so no history is possible. This, in other words, means that the people were illiterate. They did not know how to write and consequently how to read. Possession of this kind of faculties is now-a-days regarded (by anthropologists and archaeologists) as a sign of civilized life or civilization (though it may be disputed by many in India). It is, therefore, also usual to define prehistory as an account or study of the people who were illiterate (and of their activities) or of a pre-literate society.

History of a country, therefore, commences from the time its written records are available, and the period which precedes this is called "prehistory".

If we strictly apply this definition to India, we find ourselves in a rather uncomfortable position.

The earliest written records that we have today (and which have been deciphered) are the rock and pillar edicts of Asoka, about 260 B.C. It is, therefore, customary to say that in India the historical period begins, *very strictly,* in the 3rd century, but *loosely* about the 6th centuy B.C., allowing three centuries for the origin and development of writing. The sixth century again is the time of the period of the Buddha and Mahavira and of several large states in Northern India, implying thereby a civilized life, and certainly writing.

Most Western authors—historians, archaeologists and anthropologists—would, therefore, regard or call all this long period ending with the 6th century B.C. and going back to the dim past, to the beginning of man, as prehistory, when man was illiterate, savage and barbarian (anthropologically but not necessarily spiritually or morally).

## PROTOHISTORY

This definition of Indian prehistory is difficult for all Indians to accept. For it leaves out our entire Vedic literature—from the *Rigveda* right upto *Yaska* and even the *Sutras* of Gotama, Apastamba—as works of a people who were illiterate, and the state of life depicted in it as semi-barbarous, if not that of a savage. This is, however, an anthropological definition, which emphasises only the *material* aspects of life—such as writing, agriculture and then city (or urban) life—as marks of civilization.[1] It

---

[1] No succinct definition is yet available of the term "civilization". So Robert J. Braidwood attempted one in his *The Near East and the Foundations for Civilization,* Oregon, U.S.A., 1952, p. 2. He gives the eight elements:

(*i*) Fully efficient production, (*ii*) cities, urbanization, (*iii*) formal political state, (*iv*) formal laws, (*v*) formal projects and works, (*vi*) classes and hierarchies, (*vii*) writing and lastly (*viii*) monumentality in art. (*Contd. on p. 27*)

does not take into account the *spiritual* heights which these so-called "illiterate" people might have attained. We in India have been traditionally valuing highly these "outbursts" either in the *Rigveda* or in the *Samaveda* or the speculations of the *Upanishads* and the foundations of etymology which Yaska had laid down and the systematization of the four-fold life—the four *Ashramas* in the *Sutras*. Whether writing was known at this period or not is immaterial; much of our present way of life—social and religious and, until the last century, economic—has its root, its inspiration, in this Vedic and post-Vedic literature. I have, therefore, called this period (covered by the *Vedas, Upanishads* and early *Sutra* literature) "protohistoric". For it is the source of our ancient history and culture. Its actual age will vary and change, according to the dates we are inclined to give to it.

Protohistory will also include, as the late Rev. Father Heras, was, I think, the first to point out, the Indus or the Harappan Civilization. In the first place its authors knew writing; it is not their fault if we are not able to decipher it to our satisfaction. As soon as this writing is read, the Indus Civilization will no longer remain protohistoric or prehistoric, but along with the Egyptain and Sumerian (and now Myceanean) will enter the arena of history. Secondly, if this people lived in towns and cities, having a much better sanitation than is found in many parts of India and the world today, produced their own food and even indulged in foreign trade and commerce, what right have we to call them "uncivilized"? Thus, the Indus people were not uncivilized. Rightly, therefore, Sir John Marshall and, following him, Sir Mortimer Wheeler have called their books on this subject *Indus Civilization*.

This civilization is again protohistoric for me, because as Father Heras and several other scholars have pointed out, certain (many) of our ways of life and rituals can be traced back to it.

But when a stone wall was found in a pre-pottery level at Jericho in Palestine, dated about 7000 B.C., an interesting discussion followed in *Antiquity*, Nos. 119, 120, Vol. XXX, 1956; No. 122 Vol. XXXI, 1957), between Wheeler, Braidwood, Woolley and Miss Kenyon as to what this phase of Jericho should be called; for "a wall", implying an organized effort on the part of a society, but without agriculture, was outside the archaeologists' definition of a "city" or "civilization". So present-day definitions of civilization are relative.

Thus protohistory in India includes three things or periods at present:

> (*i*) The Vedic and post-Vedic period, ending about the 6th century B.C. (so far as the literature is concerned).
> (*ii*) The Indus or Harappa Civilization.
> (*iii*) The various Early Chalcolithic or Late Neolithic Cultures. These, *I believe*, in many of the regions above mentioned, were contemporary with and, perhaps, related to our protohistoric literature.

Prehistory will then comprise the various Stone Ages when man was a nomadic hunter, a 'savage', as he is called. However, it must be clearly pointed out here that this does not imply a uniform cultural development, all over India, and at the same time. What is true of the world, is also true of India on a small scale.

Thus, for instance, Australia and several parts of Africa were in the Stone Age until the 18th-19th century A.D. Man there did not know the use of metals, writing, agriculture, etc. Prehistoric conditions prevailed. Thus while the major parts of these continents were in the Stone Age, India, Europe and America had achieved a modicum of civilization. During these few centuries, the Western countries have forged ahead, leaving India still in a "cow-dung, wood, and iron age", with over 60 per cent of its population illiterate and therefore "anthropologically" uncivilized. To take another instance from the political field, while British India began to enjoy a sort of democratic rule since 1919, several other parts of India had a feudal state of government. Thus in a large country like India, unequal cultural development is to be expected, particularly in the very early stages of man's development. This is due mainly to geographical reasons, as Dr. Subbarao has so convincingly shown.[2]

### GEOGRAPHICAL AND CHRONOLOGICAL LIMITS OF PREHISTORY AND PROTOHISTORY

Going back to the consideration of prehistory and protohistory, it may be said that:

[2] Subbarao, B., *The Personality of India*, Baroda, 1958.

(*i*) The ancient historical period begins, on the present evidence, in about the 6th century B.C. [say for most of Northern India, including Sind, the Punjab, U.P., Bihar, Central India, parts of C.P. (M.P.), Rajputana, Gujarat and Saurashtra and Maharashtra (only Vidarbha), *but excluding, perhaps, Assam, Orissa, Andhra, Madras, Mysore and Kerala*].

(*ii*) All the above mentioned States (or regions) and in addition Northern Mysore and Western Andhra were emerging from the last stages of the Stone Age on to the stage of protohistory, though there were large areas— larger than in the succeeding period of ancient history— such as Northern Gujarat, Western Rajputana, which were still in the final stage of the Stone Age.[3]

(*iii*) On the available data this protohistoric stage seems to have lasted from about 5000 B.C. to 2500 B.C.

(*iv*) An exception has to be made in the case of Sind, the Punjab and Western U.P. (as far as Delhi), Saurashtra and the Western Coast of Gujarat (upto Surat) in the list of regions mentioned above, and we must say that these had attained a higher—urban stage of civilization —in the earlier phase of the protohistoric period, *but later lost it.*

(*v*) That the prehistoric period—which includes all the phases of the Stone Age—covered a period approximately from 150000 to 5000 B.C.[3a]

It is, therefore, most probable that when the origins of the Indus Civiliztion re known, this lower limit, viz., 2500 B.C. will be pushed back by at least 500 years, if not more.

With these broad definitions of Indian prehistory and protohistory, I will first take up prehistory and indicate briefly what contributions have been made in this field in the last 20 years.

Compared to what we knew of this subject before 1939, the

[3] This remark applies to all the phases, for even when a region had attained a certain status, it does not mean that it had reached this state in every nook and corner of that region. Even now, as soon as we step out of the limits of Greater Bombay, we shall find differences in cultural and economic status.

[3a] The upper limit may go up as mentioned on p. 24 fn. 14a.

progress is indeed remarkable. For after the early geologists like Robert Bruce Foote, had made the first discoveries in the eighties of the last century, first in Madras and then in Northern Gujarat, clues of the Palaeolithic or Old Stone Age had been obtained from several other parts of India. But except in two or three cases, these clues or evidences were from the surface. And for several decades, nearly 50 years, no attempt was made to put this knowledge on a secure foundation. This lull in purely pre-historic investigation was broken by the Yale-Cambridge Expedition which worked in the Kashmir Valley and in the foothills of the South-Western Himalayas, around Rawalpindi. The results of this investigation have been rather summarily published *as far as the purely archaeological material is concerned,* though the geological and climatic aspects have received full attention in the report.[4] Short summaries of this work have appeared since then several times.[5] I shall, therefore, confine myself to the most important aspects of the work.

Previous to the planned and systematic discoveries of De Terra and Paterson, Dr. Wadia, and Dr. Terra himself, besides Lieutenant Todd, had found specimens, and earlier still, in 1880, a few stone tools had been found in the Soan Valley. But these were mostly from the surface. So neither their age nor cultural significance could be understood. And therefore the first important aspect of De Terra's work was to determine geologically the ages or periods of the various deposits in the Kashmir Valley and to ascertain their relationship with the tool-bearing deposits in the Punjab. Their investigations, modifying to some extent the views of the previous workers, confirmed the existence of four Ice Ages and three Interglacial periods in the Kashmir Valley and the south-western slopes of the Himalayas during the Pleistocene period. This is the period which preceded the present (Holocene) some 10,000 years ago and extended back in time to five to ten lac (1,000,000) years or so. During this period, Europe and

----

[4] De Terra and Paterson, T.T., *Ice Age in Kashmir Valley and the Associated Human Cultures.*

[5] Sankalia, H.D., in the *Vedic Age,* Bharatiya Vidya Bhavan, Bombay, 1951, pp. 123-40. Krishnaswami, V.D., "Stone Age India", in *Ancient India,* No. 3, 1947, p. 14, and twice or thrice by Dr. Movius Hallam Jr. of the Peabody Museum, Harward University, U.S.A.

COMPOSITE IDEAL SECTION THROUGH THE SOHAN VALLEY, SHOWING STONE AGE SEQUENCE IN RELATION TO ITS PLEISTOCENE TERRACES UNDERLYING LATE CAINOZOIC SIWALIK STRATA (AFTER DE TERRA AND PATERSON)

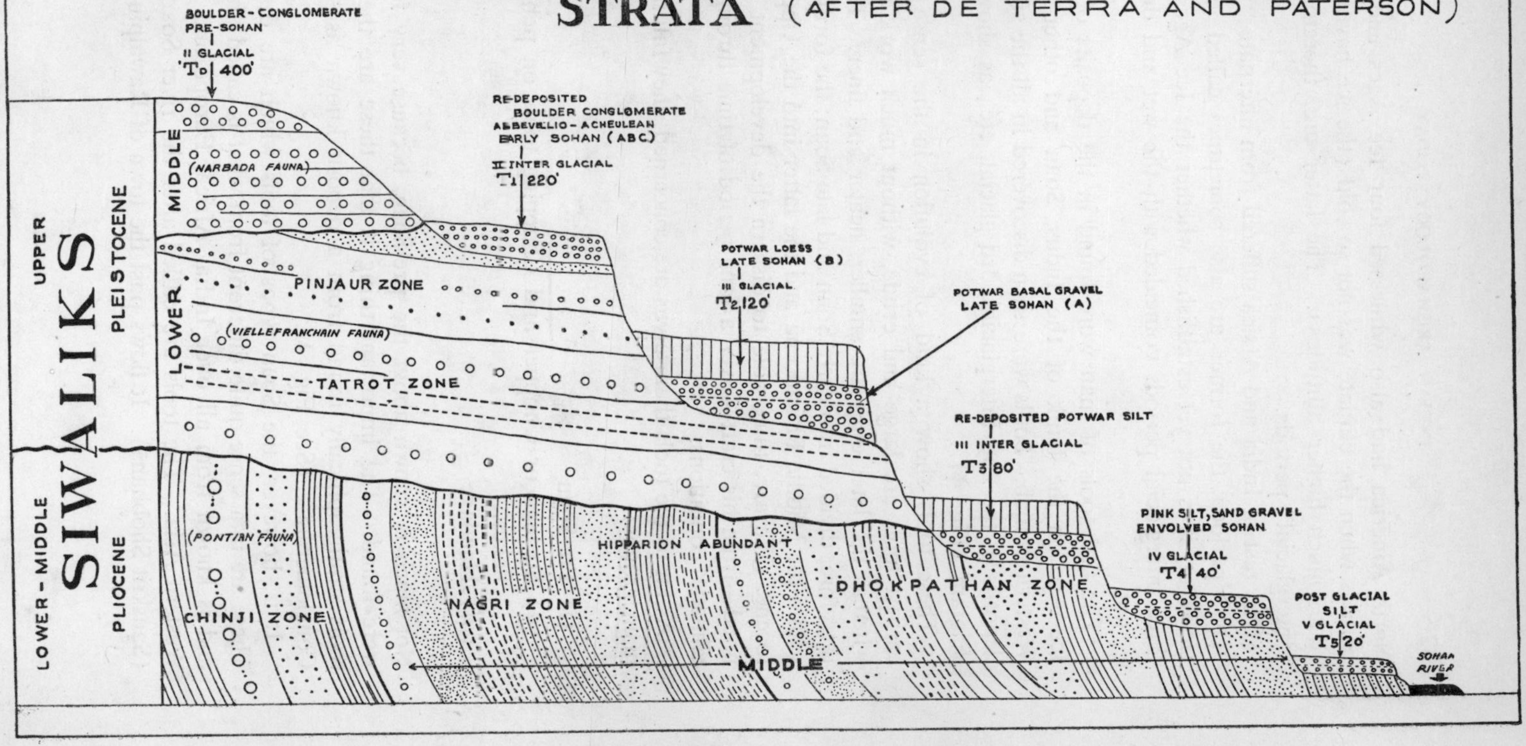

SOHAN RIVER

POST GLACIAL SILT
V GLACIAL
T5 20'

PINK SILT, SAND GRAVEL
ENVOLVED SOHAN
IV GLACIAL
T4 40'

RE-DEPOSITED POTWAR SILT
III INTER GLACIAL
T3 80'

POTWAR BASAL GRAVEL
LATE SOHAN (A)

POTWAR LOESS
LATE SOHAN (B)
II GLACIAL
T2 120'

RE-DEPOSITED
BOULDER CONGLOMERATE
ABBEVILIO-ACHEULEAN
EARLY SOHAN (ABC)
II INTER GLACIAL
~1220'

BOULDER - CONGLOMERATE
PRE-SOHAN
II GLACIAL
To 400'

DHOKPATHAN ZONE
MIDDLE

NAGRI ZONE
HIPPARION ABUNDANT

CHINJI ZONE
(PONTIAN FAUNA)

PINJAUR ZONE
(NARBADA FAUNA)

TATROT ZONE
(VIELLEFRANCHIN FAUNA)

SIWALIKS
UPPER
LOWER - MIDDLE
MIDDLE
LOWER

PLEISTOCENE
PLIOCENE

Fig. 4

North America had also witnessed four Ice Ages and, besides, periods when the climate was not so cold (the ice having retreated to much higher altitudes). The latter are, therefore, called "Interglacial" periods.

The rest of India and Africa suffered from alternate "Wet" and "Dry" periods; the former are also sometimes called "Pluvials". However, it is not yet established whether the Ice Ages and the three interglacial periods coincided with the wet and dry phases or not.

⌜ The first tools of man were found in the deposits of the 2nd Ice Age on the bank of the Indus, Soan and other rivers in Western Punjab. Tools were then discovered in all the subsequent deposits of the 2nd Interglacial, 3rd glacial, etc., as shown in the diagram (Fig. 4).⌟

These tools show a kind of evolution in the sense that the earliest tools are large and crude, without much work on them, whereas the later ones are smaller, neater and finer. These are, therefore, divided into early Soan and late Soan; the former falling within the Middle Pleistocene and the latter into the Upper Pleistocene. We are, thus, able to discern the development of man's mind—from his craft—over a long period of time through varied climatic conditions.

As far as the tools themselves are concerned, they fall into three main groups:

   (*i*) Pre-Soan
   (*ii*) Soanian or Chopper and Chopping tools on pebbles and flakes.
   (*iii*) Handaxe.

Not much is known about the pre-Soan, because very few tools were found. The important thing is that these are the earliest tools stratigraphically found from a deposit known as "Boulder Conglomerate". (See Fig. 4).

It is, however, the Soan types of tools which are distinctive. These are in a sense quite different from what is called "handaxe" and is known from all over India, Africa, Europe and parts of Western Asia. The tools are called after the river Soan, Sohan (Sanskrit Shobhanā). It flows past the town of Rawalpindi. The tools, very briefly, are made on broken halves of pebbles and generally chipped from the underside upwards on the broken side of the pebble. These sides then provide the cutting, scraping or chopping edge, and the unchipped pebble surface on the other side serves as a suitable hand-hold. From the size and nature of the edge, the tools are called Choppers, Chopping tools and Scrapers. (See Fig. 6).

Since such tools were not (then) found in other parts of India, but differ fundamentally from the handaxes, and are confined only to the Punjab, it was assumed that these tools were made by a type of man who might have been different culturally (and even racially) from the maker of the handaxe.

## NEW WORK ON OLD STONE AGE

The work of the Yale-Cambridge Expedition gave a fillip to the purely prehistoric researches in India. The almost dying embers were rekindled, albeit slowly in the beginning. Rao Bahadur K. N. Dikshit, the then Director-General of Archaeology in India, organized an expedition in co-operation with the Deccan College Post-graduate and Research Institute, Poona, and the Gujarat Research Society, Bombay, to work in Gujarat on the clues left by Robert Bruce Foote in the last century. About the same time the Anthropology Department of the Calcutta University started work on the Stone Age in Mayurbhanj. The association of the Deccan College with the work in Gujarat had a far reaching effect. It has been able to continue the line of investigation opened up in 1941, and its students and staff have so far systematically covered parts of Andhra[6], Karnatak[7], Maharashtra[8], Gujarat[9], Malwa[10], Central India[11], Southern

[6] Issac N., *Stone Age Cultures of Kurnool,* Ph.D. Thesis, 1960, Deccan College and Poona University Libraries.

[7] Joshi, R. V., *Pleistocene Studies in the Malaprabha Basin,* Poona, 1955.

[8] Sankalia, H.D., *The Godavari Palaeolithic Industry,* Poona, 1952, and Sankalia, H.D., "Animal Fossils and Palaeolithic Industries from the Pravara Basin, District Ahmadnagar", *Ancient India,* (*A.I.*) No. 12, 1936, pp. 35-52; and Banerjee, K. D. *Middle Palaeolithic Industries of the Deccan,* Ph.D. thesis, 1957, Deccan College and Poona University Libraries.

[9] Sankalia, H.D., *Investigations into Prehistoric Archaeology of Gujarat,*

3

Rajputana[12] and Orissa[13]. Of late, officers of the Department
of Archaeology have also been reporting discoveries in some of
the areas, besides those in the former Central Provinces[14], West
Bengal[15], Uttar Pradesh[16], and Eastern Punjab[17]; the Anthropology
Department of the Calcutta University has continued its work in
Mayurbhanj[18] and recently extended it to Southern Bihar[19] and
Eastern Punjab[20]. Among the new Universities, that of Baroda
has taken up investigation in Central Gujarat[21] as well as the
Bombay region[22].

## RESULTS

The result of these investigations is that the palaeolithic map of
India is being rapidly filled up. One may say, without being con-
tradicted, that the Early Stone Age man roamed at will along the
small and large river valleys almost everywhere in India, except
in Assam, Kerala, Sind, Western Rajasthan and probably

Shri Pratapasinha Maharaja Rajyabhisheka Granthamala Memoir No. 4,
1946.

10 Khatri, A.P., *Stone Age Cultures of Malwa*, Ph.D. thesis, 1958, Deccan College and Poona University Libraries.

11 *Indian Archaeology—A Review (I.A.R.)*, 1959-60, pp. 21-22.

12 *I.A.R.*, 1958-59, pp. 42-45; and 1959-60, pp. 39-40.

13 Mohapatra, G.C., *The Stone Age Cultures of Orissa*, Ph.D. thesis,
1960, Deccan College and Poona University Libraries.

14 *I.A.R.*, 1959-60, pp. 31-33.

15 *Ibid.*, pp. 48-50.

16 Krishnaswami, V.D., "The Lithic Tool Industries of the Singrauli
Basin", *A.I.*, No. 7, 1951, pp. 40-65.

17 Lal, B.B., "Palaeoliths from Beas and Banganga Valleys", *A.I.*, No.
12, 1956, pp. 59-92.

18 Bose, N. K., Sen, Dharani, and Ray, Gautam Shankar, "Geological and
Cultural Evidences of the Stone Age in Mayurbhanj", *Man in India*, Vol.
38, No. 1, 1958, pp. 49-55.

19 Sen, Dharani and Ghosh, Ashok Kumar, "On the Occurrence of Palaeoliths in Singhbhum", *Man in India*, Vol. 40, No. 3, 1960, pp. 178-91.

20 Sen, Dharani, "Nalagarh Palaeolithic Culture", *Man in India*, Vol.
35, 1955, pp. 176-84.

21 Subbarao, B., "Archaeological Explorations in the Mahi Valley",
*Journal of the Maharaja Sayajirao University of Baroda*, Vol. 1, 1952, pp.
33-69.

22 Malik, S.C., *Stone Age Industries of the Bombay and Satara Districts*,
M.S. University Archaeological Series No. 4, Baroda, 1959.

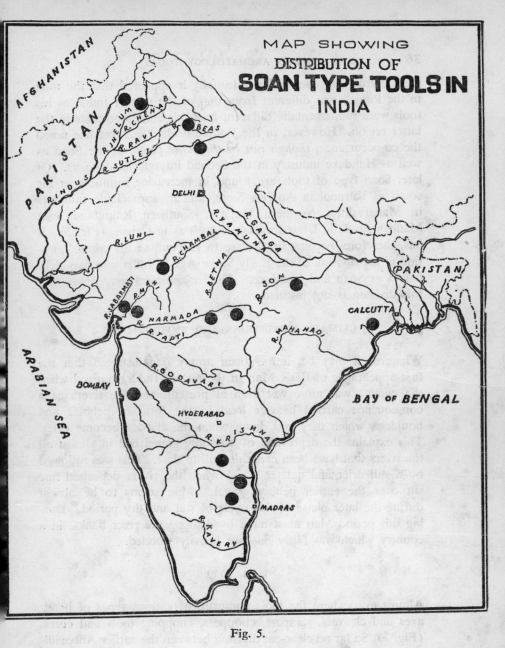

Fig. 5.

the Central Gangetic Valley. Initially it appeared that the man in the Punjab was different from that of the rest of India, as his tools were fundamentally different from his contemporaries in the latter region. However, in the Punjab itself, De Terra has noted the co-occurrence, *though not in the same place,* of the Soan as well as Handaxe industry in the Second interglacial deposits. Of late, Soan type of tools are found in increasing numbers as far south as Kurnool in Andhra State, and in appreciable numbers in Maharashtra, Northern Gujarat, Southern Rajputana, east Madhya Pradesh, Uttar Pradesh as well as in Orissa. (Fig. 5). It has, therefore, become imperative to re-examine the whole question of the division of the Early Stone Age in India into two clear halves as Soan and Handaxe. This re-appraisal may prove that this division is not justified.

## CLIMATIC CONDITIONS AND ENVIRONMENT

Whatever it may be, it has been amply demonstrated that the first appearance of Early Man in the rest of India occurred when the climate was more wet than at present, and the rivers as a consequence carried heavier load in the form of pebbles and boulders, which they laid down when the climate become drier. This explains the deposition of a pebbly gravel bed in almost all the rivers that have been examined till to date. This was followed by a still drier and quieter phase when the rivers deposited fine silt over the earlier pebbly gravel. Man seems to be absent during the later phase of this cycle of wet and dry period. During this period Man must have lived along the river banks, in a country which was fairly but not heavily wooded.

## TOOL TYPES

Almost everywhere the tools comprise of various types of hand-axes and cleavers, scrapers, choppers, chopping tools and cores. (Fig. 7). So far no clear-cut division between the earlier Abbevillian type of handaxes and later Acheulian handaxes can be stratigraphically demonstrated. So it has got to be inferred that Man existed in or entered India with an advanced knowledge of flaking tools. If he came from outside, then Africa is the likely country

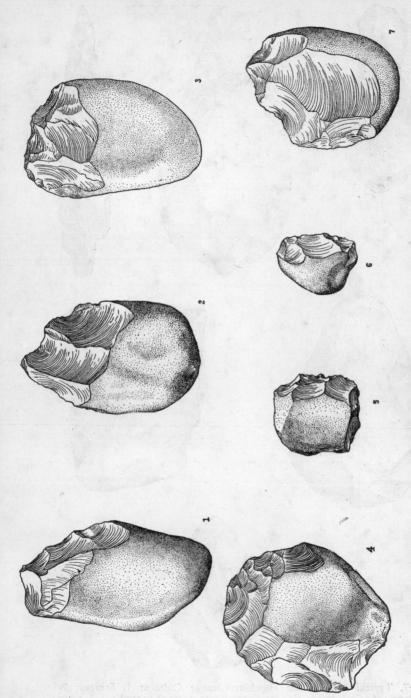

Fig. 6. Sohan type of tools from outside the Punjab. 1/3 actual size.

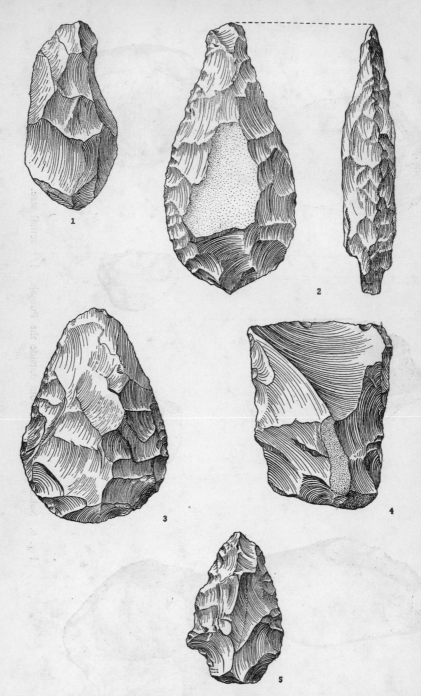

Fig. 7. Typical tools of the Handaxe-Cleaver Culture: 1. Scraper; 2-3 Handaxes; 4. Cleaver; 5. Handaxe-cum-Borer from Kurnool. 1/3 actual size.

of his origin. From here India might have got the handaxe industry including the so-called "S-twist" ovate, which according to Leakey[23], migrated from Europe to Africa. This industry also included the Levallois flake element, as in Africa and in Western Europe, as recently demonstrated by Bordes.[24]

## DISCOVERY OF ANOTHER STONE AGE  *Nevasian*

Side by side with the Early Palaeolithic or Old Stone Age, evidence for another Stone Age culture has come forward in the last few years. Its first traces were found as far back as 1943[25] at Nandur-Madhmeshwar on the Godavari. But it is only since 1954-55 that its character is becoming clear. Essentially the tools consist of different types of scrapers and points[26] and tools known as borers or awls[27] and borer-scrapers and a few blade-like flakes (but not blades, for these do not show the characteristic flake technique). (Fig. 8-9). This tool complex is quite different from the Handaxe-Cleaver as well as the Early Soan, though some of the tool types might be compared with those of the Late Soan. Not only are the tool types markedly different from those of the Old Stone Age, but generally the raw material of which they are made is also different. Fine-grained material like chert, jasper, chalcedony, agate was preferred to trap (basalt), quartz and quartzite. Tools like these were hitherto known from the surface and were therefore regarded as late, and since they were (comparatively) small, were thought of as a part of the microlithic (or Mesolithic) culture. However, stratified deposits have been recorded since 1954 (or 1943) from gravels which seem to overlie the older eroded gravel against the high cliff-

23 Leakey, *Adam's Ancestors*, 4th edition, London, 1953, pp. 77.

24 Bordes, F., *Proceedings, Prehistoric Society for* 1956, New Series, Vol. XXII, p. 5.

25 Sankalia, H.D., "Studies in Prehistory of the Deccan etc." in *Bulletin, Deccan College Research Institute,* Vol. IV, 1943, pp. 186-203. In fact, in the light of our present knowledge the agate flake found by Wyne at Mungi near Paithan in 1863 would be the first tool of this Stone Age Culture.

26 Allchin, Bridget (see below for full reference) notes only a few points and comments on their absence or rarity, (pp. 10 and 29). But this seems to be due to the limited nature of her collections.

27 Allchin also uses the term "beak" for the awl-point.

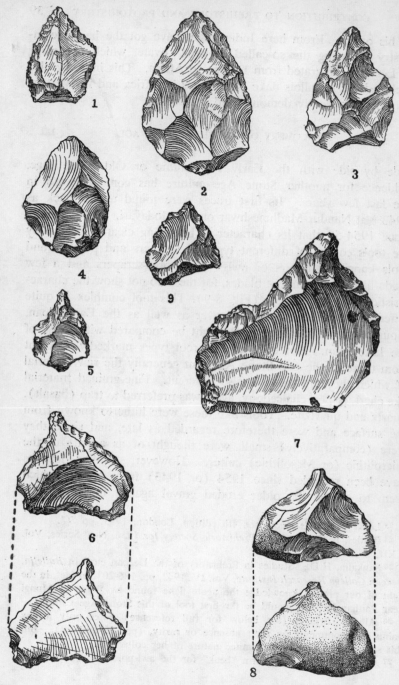

Fig. 8. Tools of Nevasian Industry: Points (Arrow or spear-heads?) and Borers. 1, 6 Maharashtra; 3, 7 Rajasthan, 4 Orissa; 5, 9 Karnatak; 2, 8 Andhra. ½ actual size.

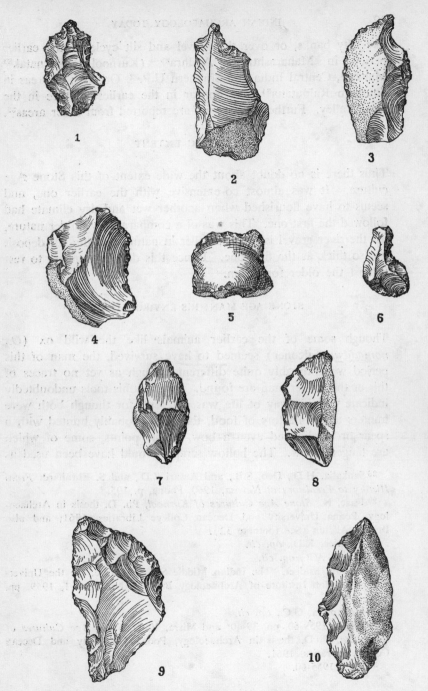

Fig. 9. Tools of Nevasian Industry: Borers and Scrapers: 2, 7, 8 Maharashtra; 1, 5, 6, 9 Karnatak; 4, 10 Rajasthan, 3 Orissa.

like silty banks, or over the gravel and silt cycle of the earlier period in Maharashtra[28], Andhra[29] (Kurnool), Karnatak[30] Malwa[31], Central India and Southern U.P.[32], Orissa[33]; whereas in Southern Rajputana[34] they appear in the earliest culture in the Luni Valley. Further discoveries are reported from other areas[35].

## GEOGRAPHIC EXTENT

Thus there is no doubt about the wide extent of this Stone Age culture. It was almost co-extensive with the earlier one, and seems to have flourished when another wet and dry climate had followed the first one. This was of a comparatively milder nature, for the river gravel is much smaller in nature and the silt deposit not so thick as the first one. Hence this deposit appears to rest against the older formation.

## STONE AGE MAN: HIS ENVIRONMENT

Though some of the earlier animals like the wild ox (*Ox nomadicus* Falconer) seemed to have survived, the man of this period was probably quite different, though as yet no traces of this or the earlier man are found. Any way his tools undoubtedly indicate that his way of life was different; for though both were hunters and collectors of food, this man probably hunted with a spear or javelin and even a bow, as the points, some of which are tanged, show. The hollow scraper would have been used as

[28] Sankalia, H.D., Deo, S.B., and Ansari Z.D., and S. Ehrahardt *From History to Prehistory at Nevasa*, 1960, Poona, p. 105.

[29] Isaac, N., *Stone Age Cultures of Kurnool*, Ph. D. thesis in Archaeology, Poona University and Deccan College Libraries, 1961; and also Bridget Allchin (See footnote 32).

[30] Banerjee, K.D., *op. cit.*

[31] Khatri, A.P., *op. cit.*

[32] Allchin, Bridget, "The Indian Middle Stone Age etc." in the University of London Institute of Archaeology *Bulletin*, Number 11, 1959, pp. 1-36.

[33] Mohapatra, G.C., *op. cit.*

[34] *I.A.R.*, 1959-60, pp. 39-40; and Misra, V. N. *Stone Age Cultures of Rajputana*, Ph.D. thesis in Archaeology, Poona University and Deccan College Libraries, 1961.

[35] *Ibid.*, 1955-60.

spoke-shaves, as smoothers of shafts of these weapons, and the borers or awls for piercing the skins of animals, etc. and the scrapers for dressing them. Man's habitation was once again on open river banks and near rocks where the raw material was easily available. The country must have been wooded, but, perhaps, less thickly than during the previous Stone Age.

## NAME: NEVASIAN

Since the tools occur in a gravel, overlying the earlier deposit and underlie later deposits containing microlithic industries, it was thought advisable to designate the culture as "Middle Palaeolithic".[36] However, this term presupposes the existence of an Upper Palaeolithic culture which is not yet well attested from many regions. It was therefore suggested that a term of much wider connotation, like the "Middle Stone Age"[37] be applied to it. This is also found to be unsatisfactory. Hence, as is the common practice with archaeologists and anthropologists, it is proposed to call the culture by the type site—Nevasa—"Nevasian".[38] This name prefixed with the regional name as "Karnatak or Orissa Nevasian" will give a correct idea about the nature of the culture, without involving questions of its place in time or any relation to the Middle Palaeolithic Industry of Western Europe[39] or Northern Africa.

## UPPER PALAEOLITHIC CULTURE

The Upper Palaeolithic in Western Europe has such well-marked and unusual features that it is well-nigh impossible to expect a repetition of the same elsewhere, for these were a product of peculiar climatic and corresponding floral and faunal surroundings. We should, therefore, be satisfied if we find even a part of the

---

[36] Sankalia, and others, 1960, *op. cit.*

[37] Subbarao, *The Personality of India*, 1958, pp. 37-41. And after him Bridget Allchin, *op. cit.*

[38] Banerjee, K.D., *op. cit.*, p. 143.

[39] Even here the term is being used less and less, for the Levallois which was regarded as the "hall-mark" of this period is now found associated with the earlier handaxe culture.

Upper Palaeolithic tool assemblage with several kinds of blades (fine, thin or thick, narrow as opposed to broad flakes removed from cores which look fluted as the blades are struck off by pressure flaking or with the help of a punch). Associated with these in Europe are several kinds of burins or tools with a chisel-like edge made by a vertical blow for engraving in bone or stone and on cave walls.

Two regions in India—one Kurnool[40] in Andhra and the other Bombay[41] in Maharashtra—had yielded a succession of industries, though now it appears[42] that in the latter the tools probably belong to one or at the most two culture groups only. Thus the existence of an Upper Palaeolithic culture is not yet well established in India. More systematic search is necessary in the limestone and sandstone cave regions of India, like Bhopal, Sagar, Jabalpur in Madhya Pradesh, Mirzapur in Uttar Pradesh and Kurnool in Andhra.

### MESOLITHIC OR TRANSITIONAL CULTURES

Tiny implements called "microliths" had been reported from a number of sites even in the last century. The list of these has been considerably augmented by the subsequent research during the last 20 years. Robert Bruce Foote had placed them in the Neolithic period since in some regions they occurred with potsherds which herald definitely a higher state of life. Other scholars, particularly Indian, regarded them as of higher antiquity and belonging to a Mesolithic Stage of culture, between the Palaeolithic and the Neolithic, whereas others regarded them as almost recent.

Though no definite light has been thrown on this problem

[40] Cammiade, L.A. and Burkitt, M.C., "Fresh Light on the Stone Ages in South-East India", *Antiquity*, Vol. IV, 1930, pp. 327-39.

[41] Todd, K.R.U., "Palaeolithic Industries of Bombay", *Journal of the Royal Anthropological Institute of Great Britain and Ireland*, Vol. LXIX, 1939, pp. 257-72.

[42] When these lectures were being delivered, Kandivli and Borivli were carefully surveyed by the writer with the help of his two pupils—Dr. G. C. Mohapatra and Shri V. N. Misra. The new sections and tools were also seen by Professor F. E. Zeuner.

within the last 20 years, systematic work in Northern Gujarat[43], careful observation of their occurrence in Tinnevelly[44], small excavations in West Bengal[45] and detailed study in Mysore[46] have now shown that in all these areas microliths are considerably old —probably Mesolithic. And though it is difficult to generalize, their occurrence coincides with a drier climatic phase and scrub forests. In Gujarat alone, an idea of the life of the people who manufactured these microliths and their times can also be had. Very briefly, these people lived in Northern and Central Gujarat when the climate was slightly more wet than at present. They had occupied, perhaps temporarily, elevated areas—sand dunes— formed during the previous dry period and which enclosed on three sides small inundation lakes. They eked out their living by hunting and fishing. It appears from the large quantities of cut animal bones found in their habitation that these animals— cattle (cow/ox), *nilgai,* deer, rhinoceros, mongoose and pig, small burrowing ones like squirrel, rats/mice and tortoise and fish— were brought and cut up in their camps. All these activities were no doubt carried out with tiny tools, points (arrow-heads), awls, scrapers of various types, blades and gravers or burins. No traces of fire have been so far seen, but extremely minute quantities of potsherds do suggest acquaintance with pottery. Quern fragments are so small that these could hardly have been used for grinding grain, even if collected wild. The hunter-fishers' love for the chase is also attested to by their long, slender body, particularly long thin legs. Among the few ornaments are round flat beads and beads of dentalium shell, the latter showing contact direct or otherwise with the sea-coast. Whatever the economic and cultural stage, they had some idea of life after death; for the dead were buried in a highly flexed posture, usually in north-south direction. Physically or racially they were fairly tall, with

[43] Sankalia, H.D. "Microlithic Industry of Langhnaj" in *Journal, Gujarat Research Society,* Vol. XVII, 1956, pp. 275-84, and earlier references cited therein.

[44] Zeuner, F.E. and Allchin, Bridget "Microlithic Sites of Tinnevelly", in *A.I.,* No. 12, 1956, pp. 4-20.

[45] Lal, B.B., "Birbhanpur etc." in *A.I.,* No. 14, 1958, pp. 4-48.

[46] Seshadri, M., *The Stone-using Cultures of Prehistoric and Proto-historic Mysore,* London, 1956.

long head, slightly protruding lower lip and recall the Hamitic people of Egypt.[47]

The microliths from Birbhanpur[48] in West Bengal and the Teris[49] of South India might belong to a still earlier period within the Mesolithic, as indicated by the geological deposit in which they lie and the tool types. Among the latter there are undoubted burins, whereas the small bifacial points from the Teris so far remain unparalleled in India, though slightly bigger ones have been noted by Misra from the Luni Valley in Western Rajputana.

## NEOLITHIC OR NEW STONE AGE

While the earlier Stone Age cultures belonged to the Pleistocene period (sub-recent), and the three or four microlithic cultures to a border line between the sub-recent and recent, the Neolithic or the New Stone Age cultures definitely fall within the recent. Unfortunately, save for surface collections in this century and the last, so little systematic work has been done in this field that no clear positive picture of the life of the Neolithic people can be had. That these people were pastoral-cum-agricultural employing polished stone tools for cutting as well as dressing the wood (carpentry), can certainly be inferred from their tools. But nothing more; except that three or four Neolithic zones have now been recognized from the study of the tool types and their affinities. Thus we have first the pure south-eastern group covering Andhra-Karnatak, then the eastern further divisible into (a) Assam, (b) Bihar and Orissa. (Fig. 10).

The third has just come to light from a site—Burzahom—near Srinagar in Kashmir. Small excavations at three or four sites in Andhra-Karnatak—Sangankallu[50], Nagarjunakonda[51], Maski[52],

[47] Sankalia, and Karve, I., in *American Anthropologist,* Vol. LI, 1949, p. 34.

[48] Lal, B.B. *op. cit.*

[49] Zeuner, F.E. and Allchin, *op. cit.*

[50] Subbarao, B., *Stone Age Cultures of Bellary,* Deccan College Dissertation Series 7, Poona, 1948.

[51] *I.A.R.,* 1959-60, pp. 5-10.

[52] Thapar, B.K., "Maski 1954: A Chalcolithic Site of the Southern Deccan", *A.I.,* No. 13, 1957, pp. 4-142.

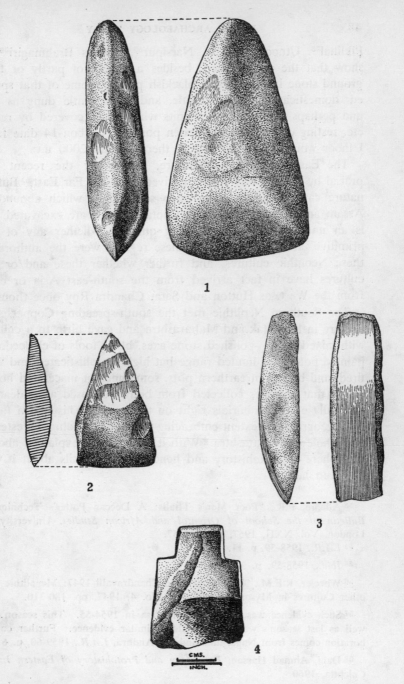

Fig. 10. Neolithic tools: 1 Fully Polished axe; 2 Partly Polished adze;
3 Almost fully Polished chisel; 4 Fully Polished axe with a shoulder or
Shouldered Tool. ½ actual size.

Piklihal[53], Utnoor[54] and T. Narsipur[55], besides Brahmagiri[56] — show that the people used, besides a variety of partly or fully ground stone implements, a blackish pottery, some of that spouted; domesticated humped cattle, and burnt cattle dung as fuel and perhaps lived in shallow pits which were covered by reeds, etc. resting on undressed wooden posts.[57] Carbon-14 date from Utnoor would place the culture there around 2000 B.C.

The Eastern Neolithic Culture, shown by the recent appraisal by Dani[58], was partly received from the Far East. But its nature can only be known when some sites, which abound in Assam and Bihar, particularly Chota Nagpur, are excavated. It is an unanswered but interesting question whether any of the primitive, aboriginal tribes in these regions were the authors of these Neolithic cultures, and further whether these and/or the cultures have in fact arrived from the south-east Asia or even from the West, as Hutton and Sarat Chandra Roy once thought.

The Southern Neolithic met the south-spreading Copper Age Culture in Karnatak and Maharashtra and gave birth to a culture with mixed traits—polished stone axes, blade tools of chalcedony, painted pottery of limited range but highly sophisticated and well fired, and burials in earthern pots, sometimes of macerated bones only, (that is bones collected from bodies exposed after death), and fully extended burials right on the earth. This had a fairly large geographical extent embracing Karnatak, Andhra (Western) and whole of Maharashtra. With it we enter, as explained above, the sphere of protohistory and hence further details about it will be given later.

---

[53] Allchin, F.R., "Poor Men's Thalis: A Deccan Potter's Technique", *Bulletin of the School of Oriental and African Studies,* University of London, Vol. XXII, 1957, pp. 250-57.

[54] *I.A.R.,* 1958-59, p. 11.

[55] *Ibid.,* 1958-59, p. 33.

[56] Wheeler, R.E.M., "Brahmagiri and Chandravalli 1947: Megalithic and other Cultures in Mysore State", *A.I.,* No. 4, 1947, pp. 180-310.

[57] Such evidence was first had at Nevasa in 1954-55. This season's as well as last season's work have yielded similar evidence. Further corroboration comes from Nagarjunakonda in Andhra, *I.A.R.,* 1959-60, p. 6.

[58] Dani, Ahmad Hassan, *Prehistory and Protohistory of Eastern India,* Calcutta, 1960.

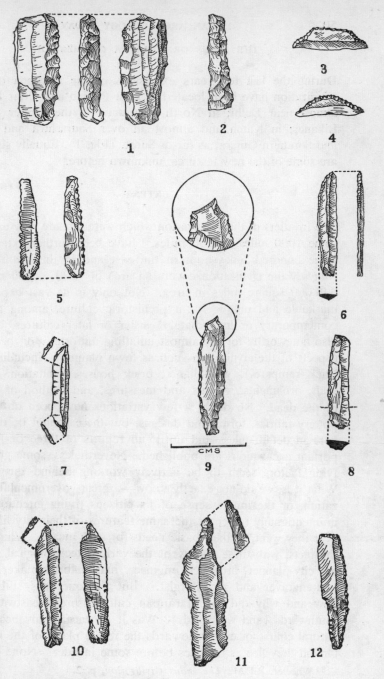

Fig. 11. Chalcolithic Blade Industry: 1, Core with crested ridge; 2. Crested ridged flake; 3, 7 Trapeze; 4 Lunate; 5 Saw; 6 Fully retouched **penknife** blade; 8 Straight-sided retouched blade; 9-11 Fully and partly **retouched** points; 12 Tanged point (tip broken). ½ actual size.

### THE INDUS OR HARAPPA CIVILIZATION

During the last ten years extensions of the Harappa or Indus Civilization have been located in East Punjab and Uttar Pradesh, almost near Delhi; in North Rajputana in the former State of Bikaner; in Kutch and almost all over Saurashtra and Central and Southern Gujarat as far as Surat. (Fig. 1). Equally significant are some of the new features, unknown before.

#### EXTENT

The frontiers of this civilization which were already very extensive, some 1000 miles by 500 miles,[59] have been further extended by some hundred miles both in the east and in the south. Thus *roughly* the civilization covers an area of 1200 × 700 miles ≔ 840,000 square miles in area. Not only is its vast expanse remarkable and unique for a prehistoric culture, among the then contemporary or immediately earlier or later cultures, but it is also noteworthy for the almost unfailing uniformity of the various aspects of the civilization such as town planning (including mud-brick ramparts), well-aligned brick houses, sanitation, pottery, seals, ornaments, weights and measures, and method of disposal of the dead. No doubt a few variations have been observed in pottery fabrics, forms and designs, but these cannot be discussed here in detail unless and until full reports of three or four important excavations are published. Nevertheless, some great unifying factors seem to be actively working behind this feature. What it is, we do not exactly know—a great governmental organization, or the innate sense of its citizens trying intentionally or unintentionally to repeat the same features of their city life wherever they went, or their basic needs for such means. Whatever be the facts, with these also went the various technological skills of the city-planner, architect, engineer, mason, brick-maker, potter, seal-engraver and metallurgist. But the questions still remain how and why did the Harappan culture spread eastwards and southwards (and westwards)? Was it a peaceful advance, in the natural course of events, towards the fertile plains of the Ganges? Or did they flee as refugees before some invader? None of these

---

[59] Wheeler, R.E.M., *The Indus Civilization*, p. 2.

questions can be answerd satisfactorily for want of adequate evidence.

## EAST PUNJAB AND GANGETIC VALLEY

Excavations at Rupar and Bara in the East Punjab, Alamgirpur near Meerut, and several sites in Bikaner suggest that these sites were occupied after some lapse of time by the Painted Grey Ware people after they were abandoned by the Harappans. In Saurashtra the story seems to be different. At Lothal the main Harappan Civilization shows a maturity and degeneration, but no replacement by another culture. At Somnath a few Harappan features have been noticed in the pottery forms in the lowest deposits, which indicate that the habitation began with a Harappan bias, but this was soon lost when other influences became dominant. This was not the case at Rangpur, where a kind of evolution is witnessed after Period II, suggesting that the Harappan culture was not forcibly replaced or abandoned, but changed imperceptibly into a new one, owing, of course, to contact with newer elements. Thus the story of the Harappan Civilization is different in the Punjab and Saurashtra, two of the most outlying provinces of its culture-spread.

With this introduction, we shall see in some detail these regional manifestations, though the account cannot be in any sense final, unless definitive reports are published.

The Harappan settlements in East Punjab are found to date on the Sirsa and other smaller tributaries of the Upper Sutlej, now comprised within the districts of Ambala, Jullundur and Bhatinda. Thus besides Rupar, which is the principal site, we have[60] Bikkun or Dher Majra, Bara, Kotli, Talapura, Chamkaur, Hawra (having an extensive mound), Dhang, Merhanwala, Dhogri, Madhopur[61] near Jullandar and Raja Sikak,[62] 2 miles to the south of Faridkot. The sites at Dhang and Merhanwala are situated on the river terraces and flat surfaces on the hills. It is therefore felt that the Harappans proceeded into the hilly terrain along the valleys of smaller rivers. If this can be proved by further work, it may

[60] *I.A.R.*, 1953-54, p. 38.
[61] *Ibid.*, 1956-57, p. 79.
[62] *Ibid.*, 1958-59, p. 73.

mean a regular colonization. Similar phenomena is witnessed in the Deccan, where sites of the Chalcolithic period of Jorwe-Nevasa type are found in very hilly terrains, which even now are desolate.

So far only Rupar[63] and two sites nearby called Bara and Salaura have been partially excavated. These have yielded very significant evidence regarding the relationship between the Harappan and the later Painted Grey Ware Culture. The Harappan occupation at Rupar took place on the fluviatile sandy deposits; Bara was built with the debris of late Harappan material, Salaura, only 300 yards to the east of Bara, began with the Painted Grey Ware. In addition, at Rupar itself the latter ware was found over the two phases of the Harappan culture. This juxtaposition proves that the Harappan is the earliest culture in the region, and the Painted Grey Ware came much later. The pottery forms at Bara show new forms, not known in the true Harappan, but found in Bikaner. This further seems to suggest that Bara continued to be occupied when Rupar was abandoned by the Harappans. Thus in East Punjab it will be possible to build up a regular sequence of cultures within the Chalcolithic beginning with the Harappan, late Harappan, degenerate Harappan, gap, Painted Grey Ware, and the Northern Black Polished Ware.

The mound at Rupar is nearly 50 ft. high, and occupies a strategic position, viz., at the junction of the plains and the Himalayan foothills. Here the Sutlej enters into the fertile plains of the Punjab. Owing to this fact, it was repeatedly inhabited and also destroyed, as it lay on the path of the invaders.[64] The several strata show six cultural periods, of which the first two fall within the protohistoric period. Period I constitutes the Harappan and its derivatives, and therefore it is sub-divided into two phases. Its lower deposits exhibit a late phase of the mature Harappan, while the upper deposits introduce near ceramic traditions.

Not much is known about the houses, though four phases of the Harappan buildings were encountered, because the excavations were limited in extent. However, one can definitely say that from the very beginning the first settlers used the local material

[63] Rupar is about 25 miles from Chandigarh.
[64] I.A.R., 1953-54, p. 7 and Sharma, Y.D., "Excavations at Rupar", Lalit Kala, Nos, 1-2, 1955-56, pp. 121-29.

in the shape of river pebbles, roughly hewn *kankar* stones, besides the traditional material, viz., mud-bricks and baked bricks[65] with which they were familiar. Mud was also used as mortar.

While the ornaments of faience, and various other beads, the steatite seal, terracotta cake, chert blades and bronze celts are but replicas of the now well-known sites of Mohenjodaro and Harappa, and need no comment, the pottery assemblage[66] shows a few variations, which might be explained as a regional phenomenon, or as the excavator thinks, a degeneration or a new feature. The typical Harappan forms include the dish-on-stand, cylindrical beaker, flat platter, shallow basin and perforated brazier. The goblet with pointed bottom is rare, and absent in the upper levels of the Harappan phase. On the contrary, characteristic incised designs on pottery make their appearance now.

Interesting, however, are the burial practices. These confirm once again that among the Harappans, the cemetery was always a little distance away from the main habitation area. It is now a low mound, about 160 ft. to the west of the inhabited area. This was disturbed by the Painted Grey Ware people. However, some skeletons have remained intact. The grave pits, 8 ft. × 3 ft. × 2 ft., were dug into the natural soil. Within this pit, the body was placed in an extended position, with the head usually towards the north-west. In one case, the body lay north-south. Most burials had a group of pots at the head, feet and on the sides of the body. But in one burial, the pots seemed to have been arranged first and then covered with earth. The body was placed last and the pit was finally sealed.[67] The number of pots was not uniform, but varied from 2 to 26. This might be according to the status in life of the individual buried, and so give some idea of the needs, while alive and dead.[68]

The work at the nearby mound of Bara is very briefly noticed. As mentioned earlier it consists principally of the very late Har-

[65] *A.I.R.*, 1953-54, p. 7.
[66] *Ibid.*, pls. IIIA, IVA.
[67] *I.A.R.*, 1954-55, p. 9.
[68] A personal visit to Rupar after these lectures were delivered makes me feel that the site deserves a "total" or horizontal excavation to enable us to know the life of the people in E. Punjab at various periods of its history.

rappan phase. Some pottery forms are new, whereas there is diversity in slips and paintings[69], which is not found in the lower levels at Rupar. There are large water-jars and cooking vessels, and bare horizontal or wavy incised lines[70], a feature which is supposed to be present in the Harappan sites in Bikaner, but unknown at Harappa and Mohenjodaro.

Alamgirpur[71] in Uttar Pradesh continues the story of the Harappan expansion in the Ganga-Yamuna Doab. The site is situated about 2 miles off the left bank of the Hindon, a tributary of the Yamuna. It is 17 miles west of Meerut and 28 miles north-east of Delhi. It is worth watching whether this Indian city also becomes one of the Harappan outposts, and thus the oldest continuously inhabited capital in India. Excavations here revealed four periods of occupation. Periods I and II respectively belong to the Harappan and Painted Grey Ware cultures. Both, however, are separated stratigraphically and culturally. The top surface of Period I was hard and whitish, suggesting a long exposure. It was further found covered with weather-worn potsherds.

No building phases were brought to light in the excavations proper, but kiln-burnt houses have been evidenced by the occurrence of two sizes of bricks: the smaller 11¼ to 11¾ in. x 5¼ to 6¼ in. and 2½ in. to 2¾ in. in width and the larger averaging 14 in. × 8 in. × 4 in. Some of the bricks bore three finger-marks.

There is nothing special to note about pottery, ornaments, etc. which are identical in type with those of the true Harappan. Interesting are the platters with a ring-base or three low legs and troughs bearing incised Harappan symbols. If the low-legged plates were used for making bread, as it is suggested by Dr. Sharma, then the antiquity of the present contrivance is very great. The existence of woven cloth was proved by impressions on a trough. The yarn seems to be fine, though not of uniform thickness. Among the animal figurines, those of a bear (?) and a snake deserve notice.

[69] I.A.R., 1954-55, pls. X, XIA.
[70] Ibid., pl. XIB.
[71] I.A.R., 1958-59, pp. 50-52, pl. LXII-LXV.

SAURASHTRA

As far back as 1934-36, Saurashtra had yielded evidence of Harappan penetration. Pandit Vats[72] discovered Rangpur and carried out preliminary digging there. Later, it was further excavated by Prof. Ghurye[73] on a very small scale and again by the writer and Dr. Dikshit.[74] The latter scholar thought from his study of pottery that Rangpur had little of Harappan traits. Since then the site has been more fully explored by Shri S. R. Rao[75] who has discovered undoubted evidence of Harappan occupation there. Soon after, Lothal[76] was discovered by the last mentioned scholar. Now every year explorations bring to light more sites of this culture almost all over Saurashtra—eastern, western, northern, southern and even central (which was supposed to be immune from this enveloping movement)—so that the whole of the peninsula seems to have been colonized by the Harappans. If they came from Sind, as it seems most probable, then the coastal route[77] seems to have been preferred, small groups arriving by boats which would keep as near the coast as possible. Whether Kutch was first colonized and Saurashtra later, or the former was treated as a half-way house (the destination being Saurashtra) cannot be definitely known,[78] unless Kutch is fully explored and one or two sites excavated which would prove the priority of the Kutch Harappan over that of Saurashtra. To date, typically Harappan pottery—perforated jar, handled bowl, dish-on-stand, besides steatite beads, microliths and copper objects—have been reported from the surface at Desalpur[79], on the left

[72] Archaeological Survey of India, Annual Report, 1934-35, pp. 35-38.
[73] Ghurye, G. S. in Journal, University of Bombay, Vol. III (N.S.), 1939, pp. 3-11.
[74] Dikshit, M.G., in Bulletin, Deccan College Research Institute, Vol. XI, 1950, pp. 1-55.
[75] I.A.R., 1953-54, p. 7; 1954-55, p. 59; 1956-57, p. 80. The full report is in press and is expected to be published in 1961.
[76] I.A.R., 1955-56, and later.
[77] See, however, below p. 57.
[78] Rao, S.R. "Excavations at Lothal" in Lalit Kala, Nos. 3-4 1956-57, p. 82, seems to think that Desalpur in Kutch and Lothal are the earliest Harappan sites in Kutch and Saurashtra respectively.
[79] I.A.R., 1955-56, p. 70. It is regarded as a very promising site.

bank of the Morai river, Nakhtrana taluka, and Todia Timbo[80] in Lakhpat taluka.

Why did the Harappans go to Saurashtra? Was it a migration or colonization or an outward march from Sind for "capturing markets"? Unless the causes of the destruction of the Harappan civilization in Sind and the Punjab are well known, the question of this migration or coming as refugees may be ruled out. The last alternative can be considered only if we know of the existence of some earlier inhabitants in Saurashtra who were sufficiently advanced culturally so that trade relations with them would be profitable. Of course, while finally discussing this point, the oft-repeated expressions that the Harappans were traders and chose a site near some river and sea ports have to be taken into account. A suitable port is necessary, if there is a continuous water traffic by sea or river. No conclusive answer can be had at this stage; nevertheless, the question may be discussed a little more fully after we know of the Harappans in Saurashtra in some detail.

First Rangpur, then Lothal, were the only partially excavated sites. However, since 1958 Rojadi, near Rajkot, seems to be another important Harappan settlement, and there might be a few more, if not many. Lothal nevertheless remains the only extensively excavated Harappan habitation in Saurashtra.

### LOTHAL

Set in a dead flat alluvial marshy lowland called *Bhal* in Gujarati, almost at the junction of north-eastern end of Saurashtra peninsula and mainland Gujarat, it may be claimed by both. Today Saragwala, the village which shelters the Lothal mound, (meaning "the mound of the dead")[81] is included in Ahmedabad District being nearly 60 miles due south of that city. Previously, the site might have been on the confluence of the rivers Bhogava and the Sabarmati which is now removed to a distance of nearly two miles to the south-west of Lothal. While this may have been the initial factor in the selection of the site by the first settlers, this very proximity to the rivers nearing the estuary brought

[80] *Ibid.*
[81] Rao, S.R., in *Illustrated London News,* February 25, 1961, p. 302.

repeated and final destruction of the habitation.

In fact, a careful topographical study of the region would show that Lothal once was on or very near the sea. For, now the region of the Nal lake marshes which joins Saurashtra peninsula with mainland Gujarat was, as was well inferred by the writer in the *Bombay Gazetteer*[82], some 2,000 years ago, or in the time of the Indus Civilization, under the sea which connected itself with the Gulf of Cambay on the south-east and that of Kutch on the north-west. Saurashtra thus must have been an island. Later silting in the above mentioned gulf and the probable decrease in sea-level formed a low, marshy land, which even now gets easily flooded during the monsoon and becomes an inland lake, locally known as *Nal*. Its southern part is called *Bhal*. Here is situated the mound of Lothal.

The area is so flat that no one can imagine that there is a mound which harbours the debris up to a depth of 22 ft. Superficially it looks like a small mole on a large body. Within this debris are enshrined the remains of a town which, according to the latest interpretation of the building levels, signs of destruction by flood and other material data, had witnessed two main periods. Period I, having four sub-phases and dated between 2500 B.C.-1500 B.C. is regarded as the manifestation of mature Harappan Civilization, while decadence characterizes Period II (1500-1000 B.C.).[83] As the mound and the surroundings imperceptibly merge, the exact extent of the town is difficult to calculate, but it is suggested[84] that "the town must have been twice as large as that indicated by the present mound".

Though small, some 2 miles in circumference, it was a well-laid out town, a "miniature Mohenjodaro"[85] with a rampart encircling main habitation, a cemetery without, at a distance of one furlong in the north-west corner, and a unique, large brick-built enclosure, which might well be a dockyard, the first of its kind to be unearthed in India or anywhere else. Lothal thus exhibits the

[82] *Bombay Gazetteer*, Vol. VIII, Kathiawar, 1884, p. 559.
[83] Rao, *I.L.N.*, p. 302.
[84] *I.A.R.*, 1958-59, p. 13.
[85] This seems to be more appropriate than "miniature Harappa", as suggested by Rao in *Lalit Kala, op. cit.*, p. 84. Shri Rao in his latest "version" of Lothal uses the terms, "acropolis" and "lower town". *I.L.N.*, p. 302.

characteristic features of the "twin metropolis" and something new in addition.

The "town", it is said[86], was divided into six blocks, each built on an extensive mud-brick platform of a varying height. So far four streets, two from north to south and two from east to west, with two side lanes, have emerged from the excavations. On one side of a street lies a row of 12 houses. Smaller houses on either side of another street are believed to be shops, each with two or three rooms, with different dimensions, 12 ft. x 9 ft. to 8 ft. x 6 ft. A few larger houses measured 72 ft. x 42 ft. Some had verandahs in front, while others had a central courtyard with rooms around. The houses of artisans like coppersmiths and bead-makers were small and made of mud-bricks.

The town had, as usual, a fine system of sanitation which included a public drain, internal drainage which was joined with the main on the road, bitumen-paved bathrooms and lavatories with a soakpit behind. A very elaborate drainage in a large house in the south block built over a terraced platform coupled with a separate well might have belonged to an important person, or might be a public house, since it overlooks a large "dockyard".

This huge brick-lined enclosure is situated on the east of the town, by the side of a mud-brick and mud-built rampart and assigned to Phase II, Period I. Roughly trapezoidal in plan, from north to south it measures nearly 710 ft., and 120 ft. from east to west. Built with baked bricks its extant height is 14 ft. but it might have been originally much higher. There is a large opening, about 23 ft. wide, in the wall on the eastern side. This is believed to be the "inlet" channel, whereas on the south there is a smaller opening called, "spill channel" which may have been for regulating the outflow of the water by the insertion of a wooden door in the grooves provided at the mouth. The Sabarmati now flows at a distance of about two miles from the eastern wall of the enclosure. It is possible that formerly, some 4,000 years ago, it flowed much nearer and at high tide, the water could be carried inwards through a specially built canal—which this year's excavation shows was cut into the bedrock and provided with brick walls —to facilitate the navigation of small ships. This would become still more easy, if the *Bhal* area which forms a part of the former

[86] *I.A.R.*, 1959-60, p. 17.

Nal Lake (now marshy) was originally a sea.[87]

Whether this enclosure is a dock-yard or something else can indeed be proved by (1) stratigraphically connecting the dock-yard with the present or extinct Sabarmati river, exposing the ancient channel—its sandy banks, etc.  (2) by consulting the traditional navigators (*kharvas*) who still ply small boats as well as large in the numerous ports in Saurashtra; (3) by searching for parallels in Egypt and Crete and Mesopotamia.  Unless at least one of these investigations is made, the matter will have to be left in a undecided state, with a statement that there is undoubtedly some evidence to regard the enclosure as a dockyard.[88]

In other ways too Lothal is an exact replica of a true Harappan town.  The town folk enjoyed the same prosperity as witnessed at Mohenjodaro, for instance.  Fine, well-made, sturdy pottery recalling in shape, designs, fabric and even in the levigation of clay the now famous Indus pottery.  But in addition to the beakers, goblets, troughs, dishes-on-stand, knobbed vessels with flaring sides, perforated jars and lamps in thick red or buff ware, there is a black-and-red or cream ware which is throughout contemporary with the usual ware.  While this ware is different in the technique of manufacture, it shows no new forms.  Some of the Harappan forms are copied in it.

However, a few new ceramic forms are visible in Period II.  These are supposed to be evolved from the earlier ones and virtually ousted the latter.  These new forms include a bowl with blunt carinated shoulder, and a simple dish without carination on a squattish stand.  Goblets, beakers and perforated jars are absent.  While some old designs like hatched and filled triangles and oblong and alternatively hatched squares are common with Period I, some designs[89] such as snakes, very realistically drawn stags and ducks are new.  If these and others also occur in Period I, then Lothal should be regarded as not mature or true Harappan but as Wheeler calls it a "sub-Indus" variety.

[87] As pointed out on p. 57.

[88] After these words were spoken, Shri Rao has stratigraphically connected the enclosure with the old river-bed and also consulted the traditional and modern naval engineers. And it is felt that this could be a "dockyard" and it is described as such in his article in *I.L.N.*

[89] *I.A.R.*, 1957-58, p. 13, pls. XV A-B, XVII A and XVI B.

The regularity in town planning is said to be a feature of Period I. Later degeneration is evident: the houses are out of alignment and drains haphazardly laid.

However, till the very last, efforts were made to protect the town from recurring floods by mud platforms, a feature witnessed at Mohenjodaro, Harappa and Rangpur. Right from the beginning houses were built on solid mud-brick platforms, and every time floods caused destruction, the platforms were raised. In addition the main habitation was protected by a mud-brick rampart.

Ornaments of various types and materials—like shell, ivory, steatite, faience, terracotta, semi-precious stones (agate and carnelian), copper and gold—ornaments, beautifully polished weights, gamesmen, figurines in terracotta and copper, once again testify to the artistic skill of the Indus Saurashtra craftsmen. There is, for instance, a small copper dog: even though now encrusted, it has a beautiful expression. And the golden necklace—in 500,000 tiny gold beads with spacers.

While these evoke our appreciation, a few objects found very recently advance our knowledge of this civilization. Gamesmen with heads of a ram[90], and ox, are indeed interesting in themselves, but also take back the antiquity of similar pieces in the game of chess. For all we know, these gamesmen might belong to the game of chess, or a game very similar to it. A game board for such a game has been recovered from the Royal Graves of Ur.[91]

Well aligned streets and houses could not have been built without some instruments like foot-rule and compass. Now fortunately a small measuring rod of ivory[92], about 7 in. long, graduated along the upper margin, each division about 1.7 mm.[93], has been found, and a peculiar object,—like a *yoni* (if looked from one side only) but identical in shape on all the four sides—may be a compass for measuring angles. With these also may be noted terracotta plumb-bobs of different sizes with or without vertical rods.

[90] *I.A.R.*, 1959-60, Pl. XVI, A.

[91] Woolley, Leonard, C., *Ur of the Chaldees,* pl. V (C), and Woolley, C.L., *Ur Excavations,* Vol. II, "The Royal Cemetery" pl. 95-98.

[92] *I.A.R.*, 1959-60, pl. XII B.

[93] *Ibid.*, Pl. A., second row from top, centre.

Important too is a twisted copper or bronze drill. Its occurrence at so early a date is of great moment in the history of civilization.

The occurrence of a terracotta figure of a horse[94] or horse-like animal—the thick, short tail is unmistakably that of this animal, whereas the face and head are very much like it—is very significant. If found from the mature Harappan deposits of Period I[95], then all the arguments regarding the authorship of the civilization based on the existence or non-existence of the horse in this Indus Civilization will have to be revised, unless, of course, the animal is not a horse, but an onigar—wild ass—which still survives in the Little Rann of Kutch and north-west Saurashtra.[96]

The discovery of the cemetery in the south, on the lower part of the mound, almost level with the surrounding plain confirms once again our views regarding the methods of disposal practised by the Harappans.

Until early 1960, some 17 graves or burials have been found. Stratigraphically, it appears, these are assignable to Phase III-V, that is the closing part of Period I and the whole of Period II (which has only one phase, viz., Phase V).

The method of burial seems to be simple; a fairly large pit was dug and the body put in a north-south direction with the head to the north, placed on a slightly raised ground, and the face in some cases turned to the east, exceptionally east-west. But in one case (Phase III, Period I), the pit was lined with mud-bricks, which suggests that shrouds, coffins or built-in chest-like contrivances were probably in vogue. It may be recalled that at Harappa, Wheeler found the traces of a wooden coffin and the bodies covered by a reed-shroud[97].

In 1955-56[98] three instances of earthen pots containing crushed bones, some pottery and a carnelian bead were noticed at two

94 Ibid., pl. XV E.

95 Shri Rao kindly tells me that one is from Period I, and the other is unstratified.

96 This suggestion was made by Professor F. E. Zeuner and later he and Dr. B. Subbarao specially went to see the onigars in their present natural habitat.

97 A.I., No. 4, 1947, pp. 87-88. Burial No. 5 in Cemetery R. 37 found in 1946.

98 A.I.R., 1955-56, p. 6. pl. VII B.

places in the excavation. It is difficult to say whether these are examples of urn burials and if so of children who were very often buried in pots right in the houses.

Normally each pit contained one skeleton, but in three cases, all of Phase III, two bodies were placed side by side.

This is indeed an interesting, nay remarkable, exception, but cannot be called a *Satī* as Shri Rao thinks.[99] For the practice of *Satī* connotes a very highly specialized conception—voluntary self-immolation by the wife after her husband in the same funeral pyre. Thus, burials are automatically ruled out, and would rather suggest a practice which was in vogue in Iraq or Mesopotamia, viz., ceremonial burial of the wife or servant, or better dependent, after the husband or the master. Thus to describe the Lothal twin burials as *Satī* is not proper. It is an anachronism.

These three twin-burials were devoid of any grave goods—mostly pottery—because possibly there was no room. But the single graves were provided with a number of pots,[100] though very often [101] (when disturbed) a single dish-on-stand and a vase with round base or a high-necked jar only are found.

Period II at Lothal is not only remarkable for the general decadence of the Harappan way of life, but for the appearance of new pottery shapes, designs and blades of jasper and agate.[102] The last two provide a probable explanation for the deterioration in the Harappan Culture. Flint blades have uniformly characterized the Harappan Civilization wherever it is found, even as far as Alamgirpur, and Lothal. At both these places flint is not locally available. It must have been imported from Sukkur and Rohri —an inference which can be fairly well established if the specimens from both the areas are found to be identical on petrographic examination. This source seems to have been stopped for some reason. The newcomers—influence or people—used instead blades of another fine-grained material, jasper, chalcedony, agate —a feature which marks *all* the later Chalcolithic cultures of Saurashtra including Rangpur, Rajputana, Central India and the Deccan (except Karnatak, viz., Maski). Though the technique

[99] *I.A.R.*, 1958-59, p. 14.
[100] *I.A.R.*, 1959-60, p. 18.
[101] *Ibid.*, 1958-59, p. 15, pl. XX A.
[102] *Ibid.*, 1959-60 p. 18.

probably remained the same, the blades are smaller in length and breadth because the cores are small, much smaller than those of Sind.

This new influence seems to have spread or arrived gradually— almost infiltrated—both at Lothal and Rangpur. But before it could establish itself at Lothal, the latter was destroyed by severe floods and abandoned. Rangpur continued to exist, but in a different form.

Who these new people were, we do not know. Nor do we know whether the contact with Sind was stopped because in the latter itself the Harappan Civilization was being destroyed by nature and man. However, a guess may be hazarded. Three terracotta horses were found last season (1959-60) at Lothal. It is not mentioned to which period they belong. But if they belong to Period II[103], then the horse seems to have arrived with the new elements. It also appears in a small terracotta fragment[104] and in a stylized painting[105] on pottery from Rangpur.

### RANGPUR

Rangpur in north-eastern, Rojadi in central, Somnath or Prabhas in southern, and Lakha Bawal—Amra—in western Saurashtra carry forward the story interrupted at Lothal. These are but a few well-known sites. As mentioned earlier, each is representative of a cluster[106] of Harappan and later settlements in Saurashtra.

The topographical features of Rangpur[107] are not much different from those of Lothal from which it is 30 miles to the north-east. Situated on the Bhadar river in the former Limbdi State, it is about 3 miles from Dhandhuka Railway Station. Often tapped, but not sufficiently fully, we have so far no clear picture of the various town or village plans or houses. However, the culture sequence it provides is interesting. Three main cultural periods

103 But see footnote 96.
104 Dikshit, M.G., *op. cit.,* pl. XVII, p. 51, and other earlier references.
105 *Ibid.,* Pl. XII, 1, p. 41. (It has been described as a palm "frond" design, but Professor Mallowan, on seeing it with the writer in the Institute of Archaeology, University of London, in 1951, immediately said that the design looked like a horse's head with mane.)
106 *I.A.R.,* 1953-54, p. 7 and 1954-55, p. 11.
107 For sites near Rangpur, see *I.A.R.,* 1954-55, p. 59 and 1956-57, p. 80.

have been observed. The earliest is quite significant—microliths in a sandy river deposit. Over this took place the mature or probably a late phase of the Harappan one. It exhibits all the characteristics typical of this civilization—brick structures, drains, mud-brick fortification (or rampart?), pottery, ornaments, tools, weapons and weights. Yet, so far, the seal or sealings and figurines of mother goddesses etc. have not yet turned up. Among the pottery shapes and designs is a bowl with a low stand and a peacock painted in black over a red surface.[108] While the design is typically Harappan, the ringed base seems to herald later features noticed in Period II.

Without apparent signs of destruction by flood, fire or force in Period II, one witnesses new pottery fabrics, shapes and designs. The earlier brick houses seem to give place to those of mud-brick. The blades are of jasper, etc. instead of flint.

New cultural elements seem to have taken a peaceful possession of Rangpur and mixed with the already existing culture. Even this is given up in Period III. Bowls with fine red lustrous surface, thin walls and a short solid stand are the striking feature of the pottery.[109] These and others are painted with highly stylized deer motive[110]—"chair-like legs and wavy horizontal horns"—the buckranian,[111] and a design which, though described as a palm "fronde", is in truth a horse's head with mane.[112] Alongside this is another pottery, a black-and red ware with paintings in white[113].

### ROJADI AND OTHERS

Rojadi and Adkot[114] on the Bhadar river (34 miles south and 30 miles south-east of Rajkot) and Pithadia[115], a further 10 miles away, tell a slightly different tale. The first had a protection of large boulders—quite a new feature in the Harappan—while the

[108] *Ibid.*, 1954-55, pl. XII A.
[109] Dikshit, *op.cit.*, pl. II and *I.A.R.*, 1954-55, pp. 11-12.
[110] *Ibid.*, and *I.A.R.*, 1954-55, pl. XII B.
[111] *Ibid.*, 1954-55, pl. XII B.
[112] Dikshit, *op. cit.*, pl. xii, 1. See footnote 105.
[113] Dikshit, *op.cit.*, pl. I and *I.A.R.*, 1954-55, p. 12.
[114] *I.A.R.*, 1957-58, p. 18, and 1958-59, pp. 20-21, figs. 9-10.
[115] *Ibid.*, p. 20.

houses of mud and mud-brick houses stood on a specially built 2 ft. high mud platform, capped by rammed earth and lime. The excavator has divided the occupation into three phases, A,B,C. While A is said to be typically Harappan, on account of the pottery, ornaments of gold, faience, semi-precious stones and copper tools, etc., the presence of microliths of chert—blades, trapezes and lunates—suggest an earlier phase or the advent of a later culture in which flint was replaced by jasper and chert. This phase was destroyed by fire. Phase B was not much different. But in it appear new pottery fabrics—some buff ware and still fewer sherds of black-and-red ware with paintings in white.

Rubble structures appear in Phase C, and alongside a few Harappan shapes the characteristic Prabhas ware also becomes current.

Pithadia had in the later phase the lustrous ware of Rangpur.

Thus already a co-mingling of several cultural forces is evident in the heart of Saurashtra.

## SOMNATH

In the south-west the site known as Somnath or Prabhas Patan has been very partially excavated. But the area is very extensive. A group of five mounds known as Nagar, stretched over the Hiranya river for some 3,000 ft. These are two miles east of Prabhas Patan, while the famous temple of Somnath stands close to it.

It appears from the second excavation by the late Shri P. P. Pandya[116] that the entire occupation debris may be divided into six periods, each period having several sub-phases. Since the N.B.P. occurs in Period III B, only the earlier periods interest us. Crude sherds of grey and red-slipped pottery with incised decoration and blades of chalcedony found in a layer of sand and gravel characterize Period I A. Late Harappan pottery, mostly painted, occurs in profusion in I B. It is now that the typical "Somnath" or "Prabhas" bowl (with incurved and bevelled rim

---

[116] *I.A.R.*, 1956-57, pp. 16-17, pl. XVII and I.A.R. 1955-56, p. 7, also mentions the occurrence of a copper celt, and 10,000 minute steatite beads in a single pot. But these further refer to the association of black-and-red ware in Period I. The later report is here followed.

with panelled patterns) as well as a few sherds with paintings in brown on a white or creamy surface make their appearance. This is indeed an important development, for three distinct pottery groups are present.

A new elephant enters in Period II—the Lustrous Red Ware (of the Rangpur type)—but copying the handled bowl—besides the dish-on-stand and carinated bowl of the Harappan type. A rubble pavement is associated with this phase.

Iron and black-and-red ware in abundance, followed by the N.B.P. in a later phase, seemed to show the priority of the former in Saurashtra as at Maheshwar, Nagda, Ujjain, and now Sonepur, near Gaya, besides Bahal and Daimabad in the Deccan. But how much earlier is the question. Will it mean a century or much more?

Amra and Lakha Bawal[117], nine miles east of Jamnagar, District Halar, along with some 20 sites repeat the Rangpur sequence. Period 1 seems to be pure Harappan, though at Amra black-and-red bowls are also reported alongside. The red polished ware (probably identical with Rangpur lustrous) and a coarse black-and-red ware occurs in Period II. It is further distinguished by the presence of a gold ornament—earring or head ornament—with exquisite filigree work.

In review then Saurashtra presents a very interesting phenomenon. First the initial arrival and spread of the Harappans. This was certainly a maritime one, yet, on our showing, from Kutch straight to Lothal or some other site on the eastern coast, but not round the peninsula (or the island?) and up the Gulf of Cambay to Lothal. There is a possibility that an early Harappan site might be found on the Western Coast. Whatever be the exact route, the Harappans moved into the interior and spread in all directions. This might be a natural further colonization in the wake of the destruction of other settlements in Sind and Lothal, etc. Wherever they went, they carried their art of pottery. But very soon three other elements (shall we say people?) representing the Lustrous Red Ware, the Black-and-Red Ware with paintings in white and the Prabhas Ware came on the scene. Whence? We do not know. But they all intermingled, and what is definite and significant is that none of them carried the art of building

[117] *I.A.R.*, 1955-56, p. 7.

in baked brick and none was literate.   Even in other arts and crafts they were deficient.   Thus Saurashtra once again sank to a pastoral-cum-agricultural stage, after the sudden imposition of urbanization by the Harappans.

## SIGNIFICANCE

A few new features as well as the significance of the widening horizon of the Indus Civilization may now be briefly brought out. The Indus Civilization has come to the frontiers of Bombay and it is quite possible that with further explorations we may be able to go along the coast still further southwards.   If this prophecy turns out to be true, then at least one part of Rev. Father Heras's forecast will be proved.   He had said long ago, before even he completed the study of the seals of the Indus Civilization[118], that this culture had spread from the south all along the West Coast over Saurashtra, Sind, the Punjab and then gone over to Western Asia as far as Crete and the Mediterranean countries.

But to prove that the origin of this civilization lay further south and then went northwards, we have to find still earlier cultures in South India showing a distinct affinity to the Indus Civilization. Unfortunately this is not so according to our present evidence and, therefore, Father Heras's hypothesis of this being a purely indigenous culture remains unproved.   However, I must say, as I have been saying, that his is so far the only attempt by which archaeological evidence from Western Asian countries and Indian sources is harmonised.   How far this will be in conformity with the final reading of the Indus seals one cannot say.   But very often working hypothesis have led to some kind of truth and it is possible that Father Heras has indeed struck upon a partial truth.

Again the link between India and Western Asia has also been supplied by the discovery of Indus-like seals[119] in the island of

[118] Heras, H. *Studies in Proto-Indo-Mediterranean Culture*, Vol. I, Bombay, 1953.

[119] *Illustrated London News*, 4th and 11th January 1958, and *Antiquity*, Vol. XXXII, 1958, pp. 243-46.   The latter also publishes views of Col. Gordon and Sir Mortimer Wheeler.   Wheeler states on the authority of Professor Mallowan that, though these do not show clear affinity with

Bahrain in the Persian Gulf. From the distribution pattern of this culture in Saurashtra and the likely possibility of there being a port at Lothal and elsewhere in Saurashtra, it is quite possible now that the Indus Civilization was a maritime one and not merely land-locked. If Indus ports are adequately explored, as Wheeler suggests, then some more tangible links with Western Asia might be had.

RAJPUTANA—A SEA

In this connection I also want to tell you of the researches of one chemist, Dr. Godbole, who was till recently Development Commissioner in Rajputana for some years. He took a number of samples from the borings in the wells in Rajputana and has proved quite conclusively that the salt that is to be found in the wells of Rajputana is sea salt and not merely surface salt that has been blown over by the south-west winds over the desert. From this he further infers that Rajputana was a sea during the time of the Indus Civilization and perhaps much earlier. This also supports the theory of some geologists that during a still earlier geological period an arm of the Arabian Sea went along where the Vindhya hills now are and it is this sea which has given us the beautiful sandstone formations running from west to east in Central India. This sea retreated later and Rajputana became almost a desert. This is a very interesting theory and I wish that some more steps are taken to prove it. If all these explorations and excavations prove the existence of a Rajputana Sea, then the Indus Civilization might have come *via* this sea and not *via* the Arabian Sea round the west coast of Saurashtra but immediately to the north-east coast of Saurashtra which is now formed by the Nal lake. The latter was then under the sea. This also explains the existence of a mature form of Harappan Culture at Lothal. For, from here, it seems to have spread further southwards.[120]

the Indus seals, still nothing like these Bahrain seals been found in Syria or Iraq. The seals thus are India-oriented. In his latest book *Early India and Pakistan,* p. 111, he calls them the "Persian Gulf Seals".

[120] Shri Rao, in his letter of 7-12-1960, accepts my suggestion, regarding Saurashtra being an island, and Lothal being directly occupied from

ANCIENT NAME OF WEST COAST OR INDUS CIVILIZATION

Another interesting evidence is that which is found in the Babylonian texts. These consist of inscriptions of the kings of Akkad and lexical texts. Among these Mr. Leemans has found two words, viz., *'Magan'* or *'Makkan'* and *'Meluhha'*[121]. He identified *Magan* with Makran in Baluchistan and *Meluhha* with Western India including Sind and Saurashtra. From Meluhha, it is said in these texts, that carnelian and special kinds of wood were imported all along the sea by the Babylonians. If this inference of Leemans is correct, then we find for the first time an ancient name for part of Western India. What is now necessary is that we should read our ancient literature—*Puranas* and things like that—and find out if some such word comparable to the Babylonian one can be found in them, which from its geographical position would suit the context.

END OF THE INDUS CIVILIZATION

Sir Mortimer Wheeler's excavations at Harappa and Mohenjo-daro[122] indicate that this civilization was not non-violent as it was believed by Marshall, but it had fortifications around the important buildings called 'acropolis'. And from this it is further inferred that these cities are indeed the *puras* of the pre-Aryans. This is a very tempting hypothesis. But unfortunately we have not found anything "Aryan" on the ruins of the Indus Valley Civilization. The Cemetery H at Harappa gives us a kind of culture which as shown by Shri Lal[123] does not immediately over-lie

Kutch, but thinks that the later movement was round the coast of Saurashtra. This can only happen if owing to climatic, geologic and other reasons the direct route was closed.

[121] Leemans, W.F., "The Trade Relations of Babylonia", in *Journal of the Economic and Social History of the Orient*, Vol. III, April, 1960, pp. 20-37. Prof. Glob, actually identified Meluhha with the Indus Civilization itself. *Illustrated London News*, January 11, 1958, p. 55. Oppenheim's review "The Seafaring Merchants of Ur" in *Journal of American Oriental Society*, Vol. 74, 1954, p. 6 ff, is very useful.

[122] Wheeler, Sir Mortimer, *Indus Civilization*, Cambridge, 1953.

[123] Lal, B.B., "Excavations at Hastinapura" in *A.I.*, Nos. 10-11, 1954-55, p. 151, fn. 1.

the ruins of the Indus Civilization and thus it does not seem to be of the invaders.[124] Sir Mortimer therefore has not pressed this point in his latest book.

However, our studies of the pottery from Central India, Bikaner and then of the Cemetery H indicate that there is some similarity between the pottery of these regions and it is possible that all these belong to groups which were related to one another in some way. In particular, a big painted lid covering a huge burial urn from Cemetery H (now exhibited in National Museum, New Delhi) appears to be identical[125] in fabric and decoration with the one from Rangmahal (examined by me and Dr. Subbarao with the great kindness of Shri A. Ghosh) in Bikaner, Though the latter is non-stratified, it points to the fact that the Cemetery H pottery types and fabrics are not confined only to Western Punjab, but can also be found in Rajputana. Thus one of the arguments against Wheeler's Aryan invasion theory can be partly met. For what happened in the Punjab seems to have later taken place elsewhere.

Thus every year more and more information is being obtained about the Indus Civilization. But the time has not yet come, when we can say something definite about it, and I am sure that unless a very well-planned attempt is made to get such information, we shall have to remain content with these tit-bits. What is required is a planned exploration in Bikaner followed by a large-scale excavation, and then alone we shall be able to solve the problem of the relationship between the Indus Civilization and the later Chalcolithic cultures of the Gangetic Valley, Rajputana, Saurashtra and Central India.

[124] *Early India and Pakistan*, pp. 113-14. He has on the contrary described the decay as gradual, a fight against nature—recurring floods and partly desiccation. Thus "Mohenjodaro was wearing out its landscape".

[125] After writing this in the subsequent visit to Delhi both these lids—one from Rangmahal and the other from Cemetery H—were brought together (with the permission of Shri Ghosh and the authorities of the National Museum) and compared. It was then found that though the similarity in fabric, type and decoration were close, there were a few differences. But one can safely say that the Rangmahal type could be derived from that of the Cemetery H.

## ORIGIN

If we do not know the exact cause or causes of the destruction of the Indus Civilization, do we know anything about its origin? No. But the work of Fairservis[126] and Beatrice de Cardi[127] in Baluchistan, particularly the former, has given us a faint idea of the earliest pastoral-cum-agricultural cultures in the Quetta Valley. carbon-14 dates place Kili Gul Mohummud around 3500 B.C., Damb Sadaat I-III between 2400 and 1500 B.C. and Kot Diji I-II which appear to be Harappan are dated to about 2500 2.3.[128] This is also the revised "traditional" date of the mature Harappan Civilization. Kot Diji (as well as Harappa), if systematically dug, from the hitherto brief reports, promises to tell us of the origin or earlier phases of the Harappan culture.

### PROTOHISTORY: GANGETIC VALLEY AND PENINSULAR INDIA

These 20 years, nay the last ten, have witnessed a phenomenal increase in our knowledge of the protohistoric cultures of what is technically called "the Peninsular India". The large areas, called *Janapadas* in Sanskrit and Buddhist literature, outside the Indus Valley proper, were literally a *terra incognita* from the archaeological point of view. These presented a dark spot until they were lighted up by the strong and sudden light from the Asokan edicts in the 3rd century B.C. Thus practically the present post-partition India (or, geologically, the Gangetic Valley plus the Old Indian land mass upto Kanyakumari in the South) was believed to be historically blank. Of course, the Buddhist *Jatakas* did describe in glorious terms the activities of the 16 *Janapadas* stretching from Ujjain or Avanti (Malwa) in the west to Mithila

---

126 Fairservis, Walter A., Jr., "Excavations in the Quetta Valley and Archaeological Survey in the Zhob and Loralai Districts, West Pakistan" in the *Anthropological Papers of the American Museum of Natural History*, Vol. 45, pt. 2, pp. 169-401; and Vol. 47, pt. 2, pp. 277-448 respectively. These have made the earlier studies of surface pottery by McCown, Piggott and Gordon obsolete.

127 Beatrice de Cardi, "Fresh Problems from Baluchistan", *Antiquity*, Vol. XXXIII, 1959, pp. 15-28.

128 *American Journal of Science*, 1959, pp. 52-54, Radio Carbon Supplement, Vol. I.

(Bihar) in the east, in about the 6th century B.C. when Buddha and Mahavira preached in Magadha. The later Vedic literature and the *Puranas,* on the other hand, sang of the exploits of various Aryan and semi-Aryan tribes and the colonization by the Yadavas in Saurashtra, in Vidarbha and in the Narmada Valley. Thus our historical tradition gave ample proof of the kingdoms and peoples in what is now known as Assam, Uttar Pradesh, Madhya Pradesh, Rajputana, Maharashtra (Vidarbha), and Gujarat (Saurashtra), though Mysore-Karnatak, Andhra, Madras and Kerala were unknown, save for occasional references.

However, in the absence of any tangible archaeological evidence, we could not visualize at what stage of civilization these kingdoms were—whether they knew iron or whether they were in a Copper or Stone Age and how they stepped into the Iron Age or an urban stage from a purely pastoral-cum-agricultural stage. South India, it was thought (on no evidence at all), had by-passed the Copper Age and reached the Iron Age in the 3rd century B.C.

This darkness which intervened between the earliest historical period and the Indus Civilization on the one hand, and between the former and the undefined Stone Ages in Peninsular India has now been dispelled, first by Wheeler's work at Brahmagiri and by the work of the Deccan College at Nasik and Jorwe. These initial discoveries, particularly those at Jorwe, supplied the clues, viz., microliths of a particular nature and pottery, with which to search for the Chalcolithic cultures in the Deccan and elsewhere. Planned surveys brought to light more and more sites in Khandesh, Central India, Malwa and Saurashtra.

In Rajputana, Sir Aurel Stein[129] had already shown the existence of the Indus Valley and allied sites in the dry bed of the Ghaggar in Bikaner State. This view was confirmed by Shri Ghosh's exploration including trial excavations in Bikaner in 1950-53 and further pointed to the extension of this civilization in the valleys of the Drishadvati. Unfortunately no report[130] of this exploration

[129] For reference see below.

[130] Since writing this we had an opportunity to go through the large mass of pottery and other finds collected by Shri Ghosh, as well as splendid photographs of various sites and classified objects including pottery. From this it would appear that considerable work has been done

has so far been published, nor was the work followed up by an excavation, so that the picture is still hazy. In South-Eastern Rajputana, however, traces of other Chalcolithic Cultures have been unearthed.

Wheeler[131], while departing from India, had suggested that we in India should turn to the Gangetic Valley. For the Ganges had given us our faith, whereas the Indus had given India its name. This suggestion was indeed prophetic. For the entire Gangetic Valley, from Hastinapur, the ancient Mahabharata capital in the north-west, (and beyond), to Kausambi in the east, has given evidence of a pre-Buddhist Culture. Further eastwards in Magadha (Bihar), Assam and then south-eastwards in Orissa and Andhra, stages of cultures much earlier than the urban are beginning to unfold. Barring therefore Kerala and the West Coast, south of Bombay, cultures called "Neolithic" or "Chalcolithic" (according to the nature of the remains) existed, either prior to or contemporary with the great Indus Civilization. In some regions, like the Narmada Valley, these might have immediately succeeded this civilization or been its junior contemporary.

However, this much is certain that the rest of India, south of the Punjab and Sind was not totally a blank. Small and large river valleys were dotted with a number of peasant village cultures. And it is these which served as a bridge between the later city civilization of the historic period and the earlier Stone Ages.

How did this happen? What influences were responsible for this revolutionary change? It is also asked whether some of these Neolithic and Chalcolithic cultures themselves were not introduced from outside? And if so, whether these had any bearing on the geographical situation of the various regions mentioned above, or their birth and growth was uniform, irrespective of geographic conditions.

### PAINTED GREY WARE OR THE GANGETIC CULTURE

Before discussing the problems of origin and diffusion of these newly discovered cultures, let us see their main characteristics.

towards the preparation of the final Report. If this could be soon published, many scholars will profit by this excellent and pioneering work.

131 *A.I.*, No. 5, 1949, p. 10.

Proceeding from north to south, the first is the Gangetic Culture. Its main characteristic so far is the peculiar grey colour of the pottery met with in all the excavated and explored sites. This is often painted in black and hence is called the "Painted Grey Ware Culture" and included in the Ganges Civilization.[132] This pottery was first found at Ahichhatra[133], District Bareilly, U.P., in 1940-44, in the lowest layers, but its full significance was not then realized. Later it turned up in the excavations at Hastinapur[134], at Rupar[135] further up on the Sutlej, at Purana Quila, New Delhi, then in the core of the rampart at Ujjain[136] in the south, at Mathura[137], in Period I at Sravasti[138], and in the pre-defence deposit at Kausambi.[139] Thus its stratigraphical position is now well ascertained. Its greatest concentration in the Ganga-Yamuna Doab, the Aryavarta or Madhyadesha of the *Upanishads,* the *Puranas* and the Epics is well attested by later explorations. Occasional sherds have been found so far south as Ujjain in Central India, Chosla[140] and Gondi[141] in Ajmer and Jaipur, besides Bikaner (where there were small settlements) in Rajputana and in the east upto Vaisali in Bihar and in the north at Madhopur[142], 15 miles south-west of Jullunder. These far-flung places show the contact which the Grey Ware people had with the cultures in the Punjab, Rajputana, Malwa, Eastern U.P. and Bihar. The frontiers of the Narmada and the region south of it seemed to have remained completely unaffected.

This pottery is very distinctive in its fabric, its forms and its paintings over a slate grey surface. It has generally a fine fabric characterized by a well levigated clay, very compact, and free from impurities, medium-to-thin walled and fully baked. However, coarse varieties are also known. The colour, which is al-

132 Wheeler, Sir Mortimer, *Early India and Pakistan,* p. 129.
133 *A.I.,* No. 1, 1946, pp. 58-59.
134 *Ibid.,* Nos. 10 and 11, 1954-55, p. 11.
135 *I.A.R.,* 1953-54, p. 6
136 *Ibid.,* 1956-57, p. 21.
137 *Ibid.,* 1954-55, p. 15.
138 *Ibid.,* 1958-59, p. 48.
139 *Ibid.,* 1957-58, p. 47.
140 *Ibid.,* 1958-59, p. 45.
141 *Ibid.,* 1958-59, p. 12. pl. X A. (The fabric is coarse).
142 Ibid., 1956-57, p. 79.

most identical on both the sides, varies from ashy to dark-grey. This is due to the fact that the pots were baked in a kiln where the heat was gradually reduced, so that the clay did not turn red, but it was sufficient to fully bake the pots.

The shapes so far known are bowls and dishes with (i) straight[143], (ii) convex[144], (iii) carinated[145], (iv) tapering and outgoing,[146], (v) ledged or corrugated[147] sides and with round or sagger base. Vessels are largely wheel-made, though occasionally hand-made varieties are available. They were usually painted with a black colour, but at times in chocolate or reddish brown. A unique specimen is bichrome, having the designs in reddish brown and cream. Painting was done when the pots were "leather hard", that is sufficiently dry and before firing. The paint is mat, though the surfaces are smooth due to burnishing. The painted strokes are of unusual thickness.

The painted designs include the following:

(i) Simple horizontal band round the rim, both inside and outside.

(ii) Groups of (a) verticals, (b) oblique or (c) criss-cross lines[148], usually on the outside, but at times on the interior.

(iii) Rows of dots or dashes or dots[149] alternatively with simple lines.

(iv) Chain of small spirals[150] on the outside.

(v) (a) Concentric circles[151] or semi-circles, and (b) sigmas[152] or (c) swastikas[153] either on the outside or on the interior of the base.

(vi) Rows of scalloped pattern, imitating a 'rising sun' border-

143 *A.I.*, No. 10 and 11, Fig. 6.
144 *Ibid.*, Fig. 7, (omitting No. 20, which is a rare type and in red ware and painted in black), and Fig. 8.
145 *Ibid.*, Fig. 9, p. 51.
146 *Ibid.*, Fig. 9, p. 49-50.
147 *Ibid.*, Fig. 9, p. 45-46.
148 *Ibid.*, Figs. 6-8.
149 *Ibid.*, Figs. 6, 4 and 12; Fig. 7 and 19.
150 *Ibid.*, Fig. 10, 66.
151 *Ibid.*, Fig. 6, 15; Fig. 9, 61.
152 *Ibid.*, Fig. 10, 70.
153 *Ibid.*, Fig. 6, 14; Fig. 10, 64.

ing concentric circles[154]—a very rare design.

(*vii*) Rows of circular wavy lines.[155]

(*viii*) Rows of chains bordering a circle.[156]

Besides the Painted Grey Ware, three or four other pottery fabrics[157] were found in association with it. All these are equally old, but not important at the moment.

Undoubtedly the Painted Grey Ware holds a significant position by being placed between the Harappan and the Northern Black Polished pottery, by its specialized distribution pattern within the Ganges Valley, its association with the traditional *Mahabharata* sites, such as Hastinapura, Tilpat, Ahichhatra, and its likely affinity with similar pottery from Shahi Tump (both in fabric and designs, particularly the swastika), Baluchistan and further afield in Sistan and Sicily.[158] Still with all the potentialities it promises the unfolding of an unknown facet of our culture, we know nothing indeed about other aspects of the people who introduced this pottery, and little is done so far to fill up this vacuum.

Insignificant exposures of the Painted Grey Ware levels at Hastinapur[159], Rupar[160] and Alamgirpur[161] suggest that the people lived in mud-covered reed houses, ate rice besides beef, pork and venison and knew copper and the horse. Towards the late phase of their life, iron was introduced. Surely this picture of the people (who are likely to be a group of Aryans and possibly some of them the *Mahabharata* heroes) is wholly inadequate. Without the "area" or "horizontal" excavation which will lay bare a fairly large sector of the Painted Grey Ware habitation, this will remain vague and in a most tantalizing condition.[162]

[154] *Ibid.*, Fig. 10, 67.

[155] *Ibid.*, Fig. 10, 68.

[156] *Ibid.*, Fig. 10, 65.

[157] *Ibid.*, p. 44, Figs. 11-13.

[158] *Ibid.*, p. 33.

[159] *Ibid.*, pp. 13-14.

[160] *I.A.R.*, 1953-54, p. 7

[161] *Ibid.*, 1958-59, p. 54.

[162] After this was written, the Archaeological Department, Government of India and the Deccan College have planned to excavate a couple of Painted Grey Ware sites in Bikaner. The former have already begun

Southwards and Westwards in North and South Rajputana, it appears that several groups of people or tribes lived, perhaps much earlier than the Painted Grey Ware people. Along the banks of the Sarasvati and Drishadvati—which now disappear into the desert near Hanumangarh and are known as the Ghaggar in Southern Punjab—were a number of cultures of the Indus Valley type or slightly later. So far their existence is known from the sherds collected by Stein and Ghosh in 1941[163] and 1950-53[164] respectively. So far twenty Grey Ware sites have been noticed in the Sarasvati Valley and one in the Drishadvati in Bikaner. But unless further work is done, nothing more can be said about them.

## AHAR CULTURE

In south-east Rajputana in the valley of the Banas and the Chambal, Shri R. C. Agarwala brought to light a culture which by its characteristic pottery is known as the "Painted Black-and-Red or Cream" or Ahar Culture after the type site Ahar in the city of Udaipur.[165] Since then a large number of sites have been discovered, but the extent of the culture seems to be confined to south-eastern Rajputana[166] comprising the districts of Udaipur, Chitorgarh and Bhilwara with outliers in the adjoining district of Mandasor. But the ware or its variants had also reached Nagda, Navdatoli on the Narmada, Prakashe on the Tapi and Bahal on the Girna. This distribution pattern is in a sense provisional, because much of the pottery is not yet fully reported, and there are likely to be differences of opinion as to whether a particular sherd belongs to this group or not. What seems to be certain is that the centre of the Ahar Culture was south-east Rajputana.

However, the question from where Ahar or this region derived its peculiar pottery is difficult to answer, unless Ahar itself is

at Sardargarh and before this book is published, interesting results are expected.

[163] Stein, Aurel, "A Survey of Ancient Sites along the 'lost' Saraswati River", *Geographical Journal*, No. 39, pp. 173-82.

[164] A. Ghosh, "The Rajputana Desert—Its Archaeological Aspect", *Bulletin, National Institute of Sciences in India*, No. 1, pp. 36-42.

[165] *I.A.R.*, 1954-55, pp. 14-15, pl. XXV.

[166] Ibid., 1956-57, p. 8; 57-58, pp. 28, 44.

more fully excavated, and some absolute date established from its earliest phase. The question is further complicated because a black-and-red ware is found throughout at Lothal. This means that the ware was known to the Harappa Civilization in Saurashtra. It may be that the pottery types of the latter are different from those of the typical south-east Rajasthan and Central Indian group. However, the fact remains that the peculiar inverted firing was known and practised elsewhere, perhaps at an earlier period, which may be around 2500 B.C. Whence did the Harappans of Saurashtra get or borrow this technique?

In our present knowledge, vessels made in this technique first appear at Badari and Der Tasa in Egypt[167], where they are called "black-topped". Formerly this would have been too distant a source, as our pottery was mainly early historical, but since the distance is halved by 2,500 years, the Egyptian analogy is worth investigation.

The mound at Ahar, 3 furlongs from the Udaipur Railway Station, is over 30 ft. high and stands almost overlooking the Ahar river. The Ahar or the Painted Black-and-Red Pottery Culture has some 20 ft. of deposits. Remains of houses at various levels have been observed, but since the excavation was small, only some idea of how the houses were built can be had, but nothing about their plans. It is reported that "the houses were built either of stone or of mud-bricks and they were roofed with earth laid on bamboos and wattlel." But it is not clear whether both these methods were simultaneously in use or the houses of wattle and daub preceded the stone-built houses. Whatever it is, the houses of the late phase in Period I were equipped with built-in storage bins, and had a two-mouthed low-walled *chulah* or hearth.[168] The last feature recalls a similar but larger hearth at Nagda and Navdatoli, and may suggest some cultural affinity between the peoples of all the three sites. As at Navdatoli again, (some of) the habitations were destroyed by fire.

From the thickness of the deposits, it is inferred that the habitation continued for a long time. This is not a sure guide, unless it is supported by stratigraphy and also cultural assemblage.

[167] Childe, V. Gordon, *New Light on the Most Ancient East*, 1952, p. 34.
[168] *I.A.R.*, 1954-55, p. 15, pl. XXV.

The pottery is the principal pointer so far. Variations in its fabric denote three phases in the occupation. In the earliest phase, the texture and fabric are coarse, and they are polished on the outside only. In Phase II, the fabric becomes finer and is polished inside as well and outside. It is at this time, it appears, that the vessels were painted usually in white but sometimes in black with patterns of parallel lines and dots. Some kind of "devolution" is supposed to have taken place in Phase III, but "how" is not mentioned.

While black-and-red ware, either plain or painted, seems to have been the "table ware," ordinary red ware bearing incised design on shoulders seems to have been used for ordinary purposes. Phase III seems to overlap with the earliest historical period when ring-wells had become a fashion.

It is indeed surprising that this thick cultural debris should have given only a "couple of microliths". They may denote contact from similar cultures in Malwa, but what were the tools and weapons of the Aharians?

Such a promising site[169] has not as yet been more extensively excavated and the Report on the two sessions' work is not yet published. Without these, it is premature to say anything further on this culture.

South-eastern Rajputana, however, was not a pure island of Black-and-Red Ware Chalcolithic Culture. This is well illustrated by the rather extensive excavations near Gilund, about 45 miles north-east of Udaipur (as the crow flies[170]). Both as regards building methods or fashions, and pottery types and fabrics, other cultural influences—which may signify racial or tribal groups— were at work, either from the adjoining regions of Malwa or from within Rajputana itself.

About a mile off the right bank of the Banas[171], there are two large mounds, 45 ft. and 25 ft. high respectively, separated by a depression. While both the mounds were inhabited from the

[169] This opinion was confirmed by a personal inspection of the site in March 1961. In fact it needs a horizontal excavation as it is so vast and holds a crucial position in south-east Rajputana.

[170] *Ibid.*, 1959-60, pp. 41-46, fig. 16, pls. XLI-XLVI.

[171] The river now flows at a distance, but previously should be flowing much nearer.

Chalcolithic period, the western mound seems to have been abandoned after this period, while the eastern mound continued to be lived upon during historical periods.

Four structural sub-periods (or phases) within the Chalcolithic have been noticed on the western mound. Of these, a large enigmatic structure, about 100 × 80 ft., having four parallel north-south walls was joined at the southern end by an east-west wall. There were two more east-west walls parallel to the last, from which another group of three north-south walls emerged. These walls (13 ft. × 5 ft. 4 in.) are made of mud-bricks which are laid alternatively as headers and stretchers and cemented with mud. The space between the parallel walls was filled with sand, while some of the inner and outer walls have been plastered with mud mixed with a little of lime.

A mud-brick house with a clay-lined pit (oven?) was exposed in the second structural sub-period, and the last showed a kind of degeneration by the use of burntbrick-bats, etc.

More interesting and of great significance is the occurrence of a kiln-burnt brick-wall laid over a stone-rubble foundation in another trench called GLD-3. It is not yet fully excavated but even its dimensions of 36 ft. × 1 ft. 10 inch. make it a formidable feature of the habitation. The wall was further plastered with a mixture of clay, sand and lime.

What this brick structure was is not known, as it is not fully uncovered. But to have bricks of the size of 14 in. x 6 in. x 5 in. in a Chalcolithic building outside the Indus Civilization is in itself a very interesting development in our knowledge of the contemporary cultures of the period. Some of the houses—particularly those of mud or mud-brick—were roofed with a mixture of reddish clay or mud mixed with reeds and split bamboos (as it is done today in several villages).

The houses were provided with white-washed earthen ovens, and clay-lined pits, some of which were 9 ft. in length, 6 ft. in breadth, 2 ft. in depth and lined with ½ in. thick plaster of white clay and sand mixed with a vegetable fire.

While Gilund has certain features common with those of Ahar —particularly mud-brick houses, built-in storage bins—it also considerably enlarges the picture of the Chalcolithic south-east Rajputana with its huge structures of mud, mud-brick and burnt-bricks. These no doubt imply several types of economic, political and civic factors. This is further corroborated by the ceramic evidence. Unlike Ahar, which has only two pottery fabrics, viz., black-and-red with paintings in white and an ordinary red ware, at Gilund we have a large variety in fabrics and types. Besides the principal painted black-and-red ware, were collected: (1) plain, (2) painted black, (3) burnished grey, (4) red, and a few specimens of, (5) polychrome ware having black, bright red and white on a red background.

The black-on-cream and black-on-red were found in the upper levels and the rest were from the lower levels.

With regard to types in the painted black-and-red and simple black, the recurrent types were bowls and dishes, with designs in white either on the inside or the outside or both. Among other wares the dish-on-stand in the red and black-on-red, the high-necked jar and basin with cut-spout in the red ware, and the lipped (or lugged?) basin and vase with strap-handle in the burnished grey ware deserve special notice. Of particular interest is the large cut-spout basin. Such vessels were hitherto rare in India, but a feature of West Asiatic pottery. Fragments of strap-handles and cut-spouted bowls have been found previously at Navdatoli, with which Gilund seems to have some contact. In fact, the excavator dates Gilund between 1700 B.C. and 1300 B.C., because typical Navdatoli cream-slipped ware with designs like dancing figures and spotted animals are found in the top-most levels of Gilund, whereas at Navdatoli they figure in Period I and II. Yet, though this may be true, it should not be forgotten that both Gilund and Navdatoli might have got these from a third source. For even at the latter the cream or white-slipped ware is comparatively small in quantity and disappears completely after Period II.

Other objects—saddle querns and rubbers, sling balls, beads of terracotta and semi-precious stones and steatite—are after the types known from other Chalcolithic sites and indicate the methods of grinding corn, methods of warfare and the type of ornaments. However, among the terracotta figurines, bulls with prominent and long horns[172] and games-men with a variety of heads—one having that of a ram—are after the Indus or Harappa tradition,

[172] *Ibid.*, Pl. XLVA, 4, 5, and 1-3, respectively.

6

though considerably inferior in workmanship. Curiously very few blades, either of chert or of chalcedony, have been found either at Ahar or Gilund. This might suggest the real absence of the blade industries from these cultures, because copper was plentiful, being more easily available. For, had stone been used, traces should have been there. Beautiful fluted cores of an earlier (?) microlithic culture have been found at several sites on the hilly flanks of south-east Rajputana. So the material was there.

Before leaving Rajputana, it should be mentioned that not only Gilund, but a site at Khurdi, Parbatsar Tehsil, District Nagaur, now in the heart of the desert without any river in the vicinity, has yielded a copper hoard. This includes a flat copper celt, bar celt or square sectioned chisel, concavo-convex thin shaped-edged Indian *parasu* (axe)-like sheets and a complete, large, bowl with a channel spout. (Fig. 10). The last seems to be identical in size with the more or less complete form from Navdatoli.

Further the sites of Sothi[173] and Nauhar in the Drishadvati valley, have got coarse white-slipped and Malwa Ware, as a study of Shri Ghosh's collection showed. Thus Rajputana being a half-way house from north to south, seems to be a junction of several Chalcolithic Cultures. Its systematic exploration followed by large scale excavation of such sites as Ahar, Gilund and others to be discovered in future is sure to unravel the relationship and route of these and other new cultures.

### MALWA CULTURE

Adjoining Malwa seems to be a bee-hive of activity, all probably characterized by a pale brown or red pottery painted with black designs, and hence called the Painted Black-on-Red Ware or the Malwa Ware. An invariable concomitant of this pottery was a lithic industry, in which parallel-sided blades predominated. Hence it is called the "Short" Blade Industry of the Chalcolithic Period. (Fig. 11).

[173] Wheeler, (*Early India and Pakistan*, p. 124), thought that the term 'Sothi culture' used by Ghosh was a little ambitious. Our study shows that the ware is distinctive and a variant, perhaps degraded, of the Malwa ware.

Up-to-date, two or three sites of this culture are excavated. Two or three are in the Chambal Valley, of which Nagda was excavated in 1956-57, whereas Maheshwar and Navdatoli on the Narmada were excavated in 1952-53 and 1957-59. The report of the work at Nagda is not yet published, but that of the first season's on the latter site[174] is available. Moreover, Navdatoli was extensively dug and it gives a fairly good picture of the Chalcolithic Malwa. This is, therefore, described in detail here.

Presumably all these settlements—in Sind, the Punjab, Rajputana, Uttar Pradesh, Bihar, Saurashtra, Central India, Khandesh, North and South Maharashtra, and even in the granitic regions of Andhra-Karnatak were clusters of mud huts (though the Gilund evidence indicates the existence of baked-brick houses as well). But barring Rajputana and the Punjab where the settlements seem to rest on sandy alluvium, elsewhere they are on a black soil. This may imply a clearance of the jungle, the black soil itself being a weathering *in situ* of the brownish alluvium, owing to thick vegetation. This is clearly demonstrated at Navdatoli and Nevasa, the two sites which have so far been horizontally excavated and of which the writer has first-hand knowledge. Navdatoli is situated opposite Maheshwar on the Narmada, about 60 miles south of Indore. Both these sites stand on an old crossing of the river, which itself is a great commercial artery dividing India into two —Northern and Southern.

This black soil—at Navdatoli, a small hamlet now occupied by boatmen (*navdas*)[175]—covers a fairly large area, about 2 furlongs by 2 furlongs, and caps the top of four mounds which some 4,000 years ago probably formed a single unit, but was later cut up by erosion. This single mound represented the topmost terrace of the Narmada; the river itself presumably was flowing at the foot of its northern extremity, though now flows at a distance of about three furlongs to the north.

The present village of the *navdas* is situated on a still younger terrace.

---

[174] Sankalia, H.D., Subbarao, B., and Deo, S.B., *Excavations at Maheshwar and Navdatoli*, Poona and Baroda, 1958.

[175] This does not imply that the old village was of fishermen or boatmen as Wheeler (*Early India and Pakistan*, p. 142) says.

Excavations on all the four mounds indicate that the entire pre-historic mound was occupied, but that some of its parts might have been occupied later than others. For instance, it was revealed last season (1958-59) that the north-eastern extremity of Mound IV was not inhabited before the end of Period II within the Chalcolithic.

From the very beginning the inhabitants built round and square or rectangular huts. These houses were framed by thick wooden posts. Around these were put bamboo screens, which were then plastered with clay from outside and inside. The floor was also made of clay mixed with cowdung. Both were then given a thin coating of lime, so that the house when first built must have looked spick and span. The size of the largest rectangular room was 20 feet by 40 feet. But sometimes, a circular hut was only three to four feet in diameter, the largest being 8 feet in diameter. So it is doubtful, if it (the small one) was meant for habitation. Such small huts might have been used for storing grain, hay, etc. as the writer recently saw some in Kurnool, Andhra State. But normally in Period II, the size of a room was 10 ft. × 8 ft. How many persons lived in a room or a house can only be guessed. But possibly not more than four in a room of 8 feet × 10 feet. Secondly, the settlement was so often rebuilt as evidenced by house floors that it is difficult to distinguish the house plans by mere occurrences of postholes. But judging from the modern village of Navdatoli, one may guess that the prehistoric village might have had about 50 to 75 huts, supporting a population of 200 persons.

In one house was found a well-made rectangular pit in the midst of it. It sides are slightly bevelled; all round there are postholes; on either side, at some distance, is a pot-rest made into the ground, and possibly the remains of a single-mouthed hearth. Inside the pit were found two logs of wood, placed almost at right angles and the remains of two unique pots. These have a high corrugated neck with everted rim, a ribbed ovalish body with one or two incised bands, filled in with lime and a high hollow base (which looks similar to the mouth, so that until we could reconstruct the pots from this pit we were not certain which was the mouth and which the base).

These houses were built very close to each other. But between a row of 4 or 5 houses, it appears there was an open space, like a *chowk* (square).

These houses were furnished, as it is to be expected at this time, and as we find in a farmer's house even today, with small and large earthen pots for storing, cooking and drinking. The large storage jars were strong and sturdy but generally decorated with an engraving or applique work along the neck. But what surprises us and delights our eye is their "table service", or dinner set. It is this which distinguishes these Early Navdatolians from the modern primitives like Santals and other tribes in Chota Nagpur, for instance. The Navdatolians had a large number of pottery vessels which according to their fabric, shapes and designs fall into four distinctive groups, each having certain shapes and designs associated with a particular period. The most common is a pale red slipped fabric with paintings in black over it. Since this occurs throughout Malwa (an old geographical name for parts of Central India), it is called the Malwa Ware. This occurs as a major pottery fabric right from the first occupation and runs through the entire Chalcolithic habitation. However in the earliest period only certain shapes and designs figure, both becoming more varied later.

Then there is a sprinkling of black-and-red ware, with paintings in white, comprising generally bowls (with gracefully inturned sides) and cups. This fabric is confined only to Period I and seems definitely to be an import from the adjoining region of Rajputana, where at Ahar it occurs in profusion.

The third important fabric is the white-slipped one. It is associated with the first two periods only, but died out later. It has several gradations in slip and texture, but the finest is smooth, lustrous and slightly greenish-white.

Though it copies some of the shapes of the Malwa Ware, its own distinctive shapes are a shallow dish with broad, flat rim and stand, and a high concave-walled cup with bulging bottom. An almost complete bowl of the latter in fine white slip recalls a similar vessel from the earliest period at Sialk, in Iran (Ghirshman, *Fouilles de Sialk,* Vol. I, Frontispiece, 4). A band of running antelopes and dancing human figures seem to be characteristic designs in this fabric.

In Period III occurs, for the first time, a new fabric called

"Jorwe" after the "type site" in the Deccan.[176] This has a well-baked core with a metallic ring and a matt red surface. Comparatively limited numbers of shapes and designs figure in this ware. It is also at this time that the most distinctive form of a vessel occurs. This is the Channel-spouted or teapot-like bowl. It is in Malwa fabric. In 1958-59 we were lucky in getting a complete bowl, which leaves no doubt about its shape and function. It seems to have been a vessel with which ablutions were performed. Since it is without a handle, it has got to be held in the palms of both the hands, and the contents (liquid) poured slowly, as in a sacrifice or some such ritual. In order to control the flow of the liquid, a hole was sometimes made at the junction of the spout and the body of the vessel. A similar contrivance may be noticed in the channel-shaped bowls from Western Asia.[177]

Besides this important change in pottery, there was another very significant change in the life of the people. For the first couple of hundred years, the inhabitants principally ate wheat. But now other grains, rice, lentil (*Masur*) (*Lens culinaris* Medikus), *mung* or green gram (*Phaseolus radiatus* L.), peas, *vatana* or *mutter* (*Lathyrus sativus* L.) and *Khesari* (*Lathyrus* sp.) formed the regular diet of the people.[178] These are the grains which are grown and eaten in the Nimad District today. Our discovery, the first of its kind in India, shows that the food habits of a section of the people of Madhya Pradesh are at least 3,000 years old. Though wheat was known before from Mohenjodaro, these are the earliest examples of rice,[178a] gram, *masur, mung, kulathi,* beans and linseed. And though we do not know how these grains were cultivated, for no ploughs have been found, a number of heavy stone rings,

---

[176] Sankalia, H.D., and Deo, S.B., *Excavations at Nasik and Jorwe,* pp. 147-51, Poona, 1955.

[177] As mentioned earlier, (p. 82) an identical vessel in copper from Khurdi, Nagpur District, is exhibited in the Sardar Museum at Jodhpur.

[178] Another interesting grain is linseed. This is being studied in the Palaeo-botanical laboratory in the Birbal Sahni Institute at Lucknow.

[178a] Impressions of rice husks on pottery from Lothal are now identified. If this potsherd belongs to Period I, then the antiquity of rice might go back to 2,000 B.C.

which have been discovered, might have been used as weights for digging sticks, as is still done by some primitive people in Orissa. Still it is obvious that a people who ate so many types of grains and had such a variety of pots and pans, indicating varied needs and uses, were not so primitive as some tribes today.

The stocks of the grains were probably cut with sickles set with stone teeth, as thousands of such stone tools have been found. The grain might not have been ground into flour, but merely crushed, either dry or wet, in deep, basin-shaped stone *patas,* called querns in English, with the help of a pounder or rubber. The resultant bread would be unleavened, as it is prepared even today in several parts of India. A number of these querns were found, as they were left by their users, right on the kitchen floor, near *chulas* or hearths. The latter again were quite large, made with clay and thinly plastered with lime. It is however not to be presumed that the inhabitants were strictly vegetarians. In the debris of their houses, have been found remains of cattle, pig, sheep, goat and deer. Except the last, all must have been domesticated and eaten. But since the grains were varied and plentiful they relied less on animal food, and hence their remains are comparatively few in number as compared to those from Nevasa.

Economically, thus, the early inhabitants of Navdatoli were fairly well off. They were essentially farmers or peasants though a section might be living by hunting and fishing. They did not yet know iron; copper they used, but sparingly in the shape of simple, flat axes, fish hooks, pins and rings. In a later phase possibly they used daggers or swords with a midrib, as suggested by a fragment found in 1958-59. So for their daily needs of cutting vegetables, scraping leather and piercing stone, they had to rely upon stone tools; their blades are so small that we call them "Microliths". These were hafted in bone and wooden handles, as we nowadays fix an iron blade into a pen-knife. Among ornaments, we have thousands of beads of sand, coated with a glaze and called "faience", or chalk and a few of semi-precious stone such as agate, and carnelian. These must have been strung into necklaces. Bangles and rings were also worn. These were of clay and copper.

These earliest farmers in Madhya Pradesh lived, as we know from Carbon-14 dates, kindly supplied by the Pennsylvania University, about 2000 B.C.[179] and continued to live on with three major destructions by fire at least up to 700 B.C., when an iron-using people from Ujjain and possibly further North wiped out their existence and laid the foundation of a new economy in which iron, minted money, houses of bricks and altogether a new pottery played a dominant part.

The question who the first dwellers were, whose remains are found all over Malwa, is not yet resolved. Probably, they were a people from Iran, as their pottery shows. This is a very important and interesting clue. In that case, they might be a branch of the Aryans. This trail is to be followed up by further detective work across India and Pakistan up to Eastern Iran.

Not only Navdatoli gives some idea of the life in Southern Malwa, but its series of Carbon-14 dates help in dating similar cultures in Rajputana, Saurashtra, Khandesh, Maharashtra, and Andhra-Karnatak.

### CHALCOLITHIC CULTURE OF THE DECCAN

Now pottery and blades of the Navdatoli type have been unearthed at Prakash[180] in the Purana-Tapi Valley and further south at Bahal[181] in the Girna Valley, whereas surface explorations have revealed scores of sites in East and West Khandesh. This leaves little doubt that contemporary with Malwa, this region was inhabited. And now the question is "Are these cultures of the Deccan in any way earlier than those of Malwa? Has the culture movement been from north-south or south-north or was it two-way *all the time?*"

Till now we do not know the main focus of the Malwa Chalcolithic Culture. It would, however, appear that it had reached its fullest expression as far south as the Narmada, but its outliers had crossed the Tapi-Girna Valleys and reached as far[182] as the

[179] The earliest carbon-14 date is 3,503 ± 128. Stratigraphically this belongs to Period III. It is, therefore, presumed that the first two phases, having several floor-levels, might go back to this date.

[180] *I.A.R.*, 1954-55, p. 13.

[181] *I.A.R.*, 1956-57, p. 17.

[182] Our very recent (March 1961) excavations at Chandoli, some 40 miles north of Poona, show that its elements with a dagger or a spear having an antennae and mid-rib had gone for south.

Pravara-Godavari, where it met another Chalcolithic Culture which had spread all over the Deccan and Mysore plateaux. Again we do not know the source of this culture, but it seems to have its roots in the purely Neolithic Cultures of south-east India.

If the evidence from Daimabad near Belapur, Ahmadnagar District, is any guide, it appears that the first wave of Central Indian Culture which reached the Narmada in about 1500-1700 B.C. had also arrived in the Deccan and laid itself upon the earlier Deccan Culture.

However, the indigenous culture survived and seems to have contained the further expansion of this northern influence, and later became the main force in the Deccan. It is in this way that we can explain the differences in pottery fabrics and design between Nevasa and Daimabad[183], which are not more than 15 miles distant from each other, and lie on the Pravara.

With this preface let us see the main features of these cultures. So far, except for Nevasa, none has been described in full; so it is not possible to go into details. The information is reviewed under the following heads:

  i  Nature of the habitation
  ii  Household vessels, furniture
  iii  Dress, ornaments
  iv  Tools and weapons
  v  Disposal of the dead
  vi  Economic stage.   General.

(i)  *Nature of Habitation*

Whether it be Malwa, Khandesh, Maharashtra or Mysore-Karnatak, the earliest remains of the habitation are found on a black soil. This today forms the surface (virgin) soil in many parts of the regions mentioned above. It is believed to be the weathering *in situ* of the underlying yellowish silt deposited by the river when it aggraded in Middle Pleistocene times. The weathering was caused by thick vegetation as a result of a damper climatic phase. Thus when the Chalcolithic people entered the river valleys, there must have been thick forests. Clearings overlooking the river, or not far from the river were effected with

183 *I.A.R.*, 1958-59, p. 15.

their stone and copper tools. Though none of these early settlements is fully excavated, it would appear that these elevated black-topped terraces were not very extensive, though fairly large for the times. At a time, each settlement might accommodate 50 to 100 closely-set houses (huts). Each hut would be normally about 10 ft. by 9 ft, though at Navdatoli we had huts smaller or larger than this. These huts were square, rectangular or round. They were constructed with round undressed wooden posts, about 3 inches in diameter (at Nevasa, Diamabad). The walls were of mud, whereas the roofs were probably flat or slightly sloping, —and made of interwoven bamboo matting, dry leaves, etc., and covered with mud. The floors were made either with a mixture of sand, gravel and clay, or burnt debris (of a previous habitation) and often plastered with lime which was sometimes carried up to the wall.

These houses were largely furnished with large and small storage jars, other vessels of daily and special use, a hearth, and a boat-shaped saddle quern for pounding grains, etc. No intact hearth has yet been reported from the Deccan[184] or Khandesh, but in Malwa and Southern Rajputana these were either like a large hollow cylinder open at one side, or three-mouthed. The latter might be of a larger house, or a house where two or three things were cooked simultaneously.

### (ii) Household Vessels, Furniture

No other remains of household goods or furniture like cots, wooden stools, (if there were any?) have come to light, probably because these were invariably of wood and have perished. In pottery, dish (*thalis*) are conspicuous by their absence. Of the most common occurrence—in varied sizes, from about 2 in. to 10 in. and more in height—are bowls (*vatis*) and vessels (*lotas* or *tambya*) for storing and pouring liquids, having sharp angular walls and necks and long tubular spouts. The matt red surface of these are painted in black with most monotonous geometric designs consisting of hatched, triangles, square or rectangles, oblique dashes, etc. But this monotony is relieved at Nevasa by two unique specimens of realistic delineation of a deer and a dog

[184] This year (1960-61) a number of small circular or square burnt mud-walled enclosure, supported by stones were found at Nevasa.

or dog-like animal, (see Frontispiece) for the like of which one has to recall the Upper Palaeolithic cave art of Western Europe. The largest storage jar was about 4 ft. in height and 3 ft. in girth, and decorated with finger-tip decoration.

### (iii) Dress, Ornaments

Nor can we form any idea of the dress. But recent evidence from Nevasa and also from Chandoli suggests that spinning of cotton and even (wild) silk was known. Presumably, then, garments of both these materials must have been made.

Among ornaments, by far the commonest are beads of semi-precious stones such as agate, amazonite, amethyst, carnelian, chalcedony, crystal, coral, shell steatite, chalk or faience, terracotta, and less frequently of copper and rarely of gold. All these were certainly strung into necklaces of which an almost complete example, round the neck of a dead child was found at Nevasa in 1960. Silver seems to be completely unknown. Bangles were of the simplest type, and generally of copper, burnt clay and bone or ivory. Rings were worn on figures of the hand.

### (iv) Tools and Weapons

Until this year (1960-61) no intact examples of weapons had been found. It was therefore presumed that among the large number of products of the chalcedony blade industry, those which are called 'points', with or without tang, were probably used as arrowheads. (Fig. 11). Whether there were any of copper is impossible to say in the absence of any evidence. So also the flat copper axes were certainly hafted and used as weapons of offense. (In India, a *parasu* has long since been regarded as such a weapon). Round balls of various sizes (3-inch to ½-inch) of stone-quartz and quartzite—might have served as sling stones. These few things—arrows, axe, sling balls—perhaps give a very inadequate idea of the armoury of the Chalcolithic people. The total absence of the sword and the dagger is, perhaps, due to the real non-existence of such advanced weapons, or may be explained by lack of large excavations. At Navdatoli, thus, a fragment of a dagger or a sword with a raised mid-rib was found in 1958-59 from the deposits of Period III[185], whereas at Jorwe, swords are supposed

185 See, *Illustrated London News*, September 5, 1959.

to have been found, but melted away! The latter explanation was further confirmed by the discovery (in 1961) of a 7-inch dagger or spear-head with a faint mid-rib and flat antennae from Chandoli.[186] This is the first stratified occurrence of such a weapon in India.

Chalcedony blades supplied the most common tools like knives, with a single edge (penknife blade) or double edge (parallel sided blade), sickles (lunates and obliquely blunted points, and backed blades), awls or borers (thick elongated points) and scrapers. (Fig. 11).

Heavier tools like those of the carpenter and wood-cutter were made of dolerite and copper and known as polished axe (various types), chisel, adze, copper chisel, poker and axe. The copper axes are all of the flat type, with slightly tapering sides and straight, convex or flaring edges. One type, however, had a shoulder as a fragment from Navdatoli suggests. These are certainly primitive[187] when compared with those from Western Asia which have a socket for hafting (in one piece with the blade). The polished stone axes are also of the pointed butt type with biconvex or lenticular section and a slightly convex or straight edge.

In addition to these, there was a thick-sided ringstone, which might have been used as a macehead, but more probably as the weight of a digging stick for ploughing. These are of infrequent occurrence in the Deccan and probably indicate, along with the rarity of boat-shaped querns, that the cultivated grains were not the main source of food. However, some sort of grain (*Jwari*, a kind of millet) was eaten, as suggested by the presence of millet oil used in anointing the child (before—or after?—its death). The grains were crushed or pounded with plano-convex rubber stones, a number of which have been found, having their flat side pecked for, or made by, rubbing.

Identification of bones of animals recovered from Nevasa and Maski alone are available. Here again we have no very detailed reports regarding the age of the animals, but at Maski[188] the

---

[186] See pl. and Robert, Heine-Geldern in *Man*, No. 151, Vol., LVI, p. 136, 1956.

[187] See, on its effectiveness, Wheeler, Mortimer, *The Indus Civilization*, p. 53.

[188] Bhola Nath, "Maski 1954" *A.I.* No. 13, 1957, pp. 123, 125.

majority of the bones were of young ones. Within these limitations however, it can be said that these included smaller, humpless, short-horned variety of cow or ox (*Bos indicus* Linnaeus or the zebu), the domesticated cattle, sheep and goat, buffalo, beside possibly snails (Banded Pond-snail, *viviparus bengalensis*) and mussels (*Parreyssia sp.*) .

At Nevasa, in addition to these animals, deer was also eaten. Thus we may say that beef, mutton, pork[189] and venison fresh water gastropods and land snails and possibly river fish formed the principal non-vegetarian diet of the people. To this, we should add jungle fruits and berries and uncultivated grains though no remains of the last two have yet been found in any excavation in the Deccan. Hunting and animal grazing thus formed the main economy of life.

*(v)  Disposal of the Dead*

Burial within the house floor or outside was the prevalent custom for disposing of the dead. The children without exception were buried in a wide-mouthed earthen pot (known as urn). If more than one, the urns were placed facing mouth to mouth. Instances of the use of three urns is seen both at Nevasa and Daimabad. At both these sites, the urns were kept horizontally on their sides after digging a shallow pit. But at Brahmagiri they were placed in a vertical position and their mouth covered by the bottom of another urn or vessel.

From close observation of a few excellent remains, it appears that a child's skeleton was either exposed and later the surviving parts were collected and buried, or it was cut up after death and distributed over the two urns, the one on the north having the head and the other on the south containing ribs, legs, etc.

Older children and persons over 14, that is adults and adolescents, were buried full length in a large jar; if the latter was found to be short, another pot was used for covering the knees. The

Apparently there is a contradiction when it is said that Maski remains are of humpless variety, but included on p. 123 under the domestic humped cattle (the Zebu or *Bos indicus* Linnaeus).

[189] Sankalia, Deo, Ansari and Ehrhardt, *Nevasa*, p. 531. The statement on p. xv of this work, that pork (pig's flesh) was also eaten is wrong. Pig's bone are also absent from Piklihal. For reference see below footnote 191a.

exact position varies. In burial 10, the dead body rested on the back, with the head to the left, the knees slightly drawn up and also turned to the left. In burial 19 of an older child (10 years) the position was similar, but the hands were crossed over the breast, and the head was considerably turned towards the right and upwards. Sometimes, as noticed at Nevasa, in 1959-60, the body lying in an extended position was covered by no less than five pots. Naturally, one side was broken for the purpose. In rare cases, the body was placed on the bare ground after thinly plastering it with lime.

The children as well as the adults were often provided with bowls and spouted pots and beads or necklaces of copper and carnelian. In one instance last year, a copper necklace was found on the neck of a child, strung on silk and cotton threads.[190] From the examination of the necklace it also appears that the child's body was smeared or anointed with cow-dung and a kind of millet oil.

Thus though burial was the principal method, owing to varying needs of the situation, family or settlement, or the customs of the tribes, certain differences existed which fall into five or six groups as follows:

### Child Burial

I Vertical (e.g. Brahmagiri)
II Horizontal
    (a) Single urn
    (b) Double urn
    (c) Triple urn

### Adult Burial

I Laid extended in
    (a) Single large urn or jar
    (b) Double jars
    (c) Five jars covering the body
    (d) Laid on the lime-coated black soil or directly on the black soil

---

[190] In this season's excavation at Chandoli, a part of a small copper bead necklace retains the thread. These might be of silk and cotton.

It is worth inquiring how far these burial practices were responsible for moulding the habits of the Megalithic people who succeeded the Chalcolithic in South India, Mysore-Karnatak, Andhra. Their pottery is, of course, basically different, but the use of sarcophagi—huge pottery urns with legs and lids—might have something to do with the urns of the preceding period.

Another important point that needs to be posed, but which cannot be settled is this. So far only the Chalcolithic cultures of Mysore and the Deccan (including Khandesh) have given us an idea of the burial practices. We do not yet know how the people of this phase disposed of their dead in Malwa, Rajputana and Saurashtra (though it is now ascertained that at least one group practised burial in the Harappa Civilization). So it is possible that this was a purely Neolithic practice which was adopted by the southward-moving copper-using people.

Who were this people racially? The skeletons from Brahmagiri, Bahal, Daimabad, have not yet been studied; those from Nevasa are insufficient to give a more positive picture.

Out of thirty burials found at Nevasa (1954-56) there were three of persons whose ages have been calculated to be 6, 10 and 20 (or between 17 and 24), the last being that of a woman. In this case alone it is possible to conjecture about the racial type of the person. From the prognathy, broad face with a wide nose (?) and long, narrow head, Professor Ehrhardt is reminded of the characteristics of the primitive people in the jungles of the Deccan.[191] The prognathy is seen in the other two skeletons as well. Thus there is a great possibility that at least a section of the Nevasa population was of a primitive racial type.[191a]

*(vi) Economic Stage: General*

Whatever it be, economically they seem to have been in a pastoral-cum-hunting-cum-agricultural stage, living in small vil-

[191] In *From History to Prehistory at Nevasa*, p. 520.

[191a] Confirmation of all or many of these practices and a few additional details about the way of life during the Neolithic period is provided by small trial excavations at Piklihal, Raichur District, by Allchin, F. R., "Piklihal Excavations" *Andhra Pradesh Government Archaeological Series No.* 1, Hyderabad, 1960 (Published actually November 1961). A copy of this report the writer got at the galley stage owing to the courtesy of the Director, Andhra Pradesh Department of Archaeology.

lages with closely set houses along the river bank. Stone still served them in various ways in all walks of life, copper being rare. This kind of life persisted until it was suddenly changed by a new wave of people, from the north and the south, who came with a knowledge of iron, agriculture and town planning in about the 4th century B.C. though at Nevasa there is a break.

### SIGNIFICANCE OF THE NEW DISCOVERIES

We may now pause for a time and briefly discuss the significance of these new discoveries in the Gangetic Valley, Central India, Rajputana, Saurashtra and the Deccan.

While the economic stage at which the bearers of these Calcolithic cultures were is fairly well understood, as yet we have no idea who these people were, in the absence of written records from any of these excavations. The skeletal material, though available in some quantity from the Deccan sites, is inadequate for venturing an opinion about the racial types of the people.

It has however been suggested by Professor Haimendorf[192] that the ancestors of some of the primitive or aboriginal tribes—now confined to the forests and hills of Madhya Pradesh, Orissa, Bihar and Andhra, tribes like the Gonds, Baigas of Bastar or the Oraons and Savaras of Chota Nagpur or the Chenchus of Kurnool —might be the authors of the Neolithic Cultures of Andhra-Karnatak. In the same way it might be held that the Bhils and Mundas who are supposed to be some of the Kolarian tribes from the north-west, driven now to their present forest-habitat by the Aryan speaking people, might have been the bearers of the various Chalcolithic Cultures of Rajputana, Central India and the Deccan. In fact, our *Puranas* and other literature do speak of Bhillas, Nishadas, Pulindas, (even Andhras) and other tribes as inhabiting these regions. However, these references are admittedly late, much later than the Neolithic Cultures which are about 2000 B.C. The second difficulty is that though all these tribes are in varying stages of hunting and food-collecting stage, practising primitive agriculture by burning forest enclaves and ignorant of the real art of ploughing, still none of these have any knowledge of fine

[192] Presidential Address. *Proceedings, 37th Indian Science Congress,* Part II, p. 176.

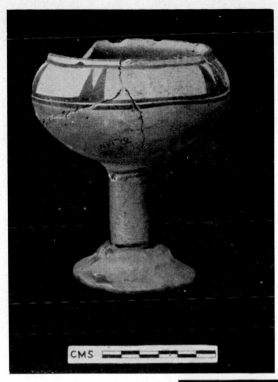

(*a*) Pedestalled cup from Navdatoli, Madhya Pradesh, c. 1500 B.C. (*see* p. 85).

(*b*) Pedestalled cup, unpainted from Navdatoli, Madhya Pradesh, c. 1500 B.C. (*see* p. 85)

Pl. II

(*a*) Channel-spouted bowl from Navdatoli, Madhya
Pradesh, c. 1300 B.C. (*see* p. 86)

(*b*) Channel-spouted bowl in copper from Khurdi, now
in Sardar Museum, Jodhpur, Rajasthan. (*see* p. 90)

Pl. III

(a) Spouted pot from Nevasa,
District Ahmednagar, Ma-
harashtra, c. 1100 B.C. (see
p. 90)

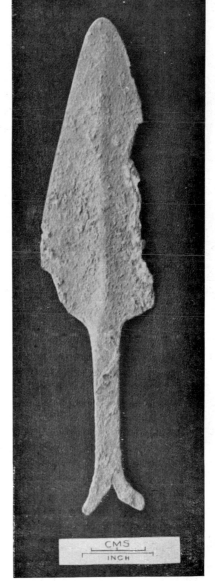

(b) Copper dagger with an-
tennae-shaped hilt from
Chandoli, District Poona,
c. 1100 B.C. (see p. 92)

Pl. IV

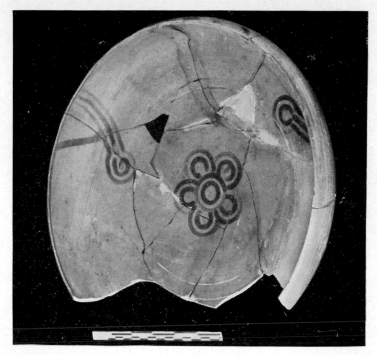

(a) Dish, Painted Grey Ware from Ahichchatra, District Raibareilley, U.P., c. 1000 B.C. (see p. 75)

(b) Bowl, Painted Grey Ware from Panipat, Delhi, c. 1000 B.C. (see p. 75)

Pl. V

(a) Stone Cist with ante-chamber and remnants of a stone circle from Tayinipatti, Pudukottai, Madras. (see p. 101)

(b) View of a Dolmenoid Cist with a terracotta sarcophagus and pottery, surrounded by a stone circle from Kavanur, Chingleput District, Madras. (see p. 101).

Pl. VI

Billingual inscriptions of Asoka from Kandahar,
Afghanistan. Top-Greek; bottom-Aramaic. *(see* p. 109)

Pl. VII

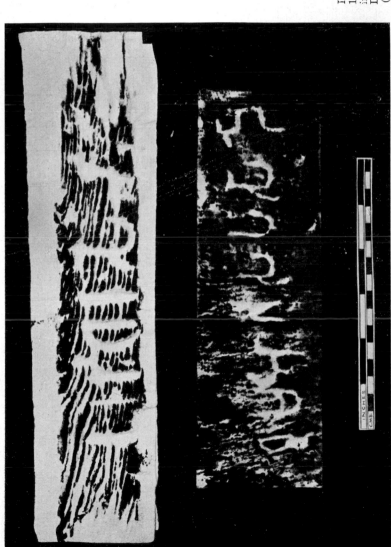

Inscription in early Brahmi (c. 100 B.C.) on the wooden beam in the Chaitya cave at Bhaja, District Poona, Maharashtra. (see p. 117)

Pl. VIII

(*a*) Terracotta Buddha head in Gandhara style from Devnimori stupa, District Sabarkantha, Gujarat, c. 400 A.D. (*see* p. 116)

(*b*) Terracotta floral medallion from Devnimori stupa, District Sabarkantha, Gujarat, c 400 A.D. (*see* p. 116)

Pl. IX

Tantric deities: Lokesvara (upper niche); Jambhala
(lower niche) from Monastery I, Ratnagiri, District
Cuttack, Orissa, c. 900 A.D. (*see* pp. 117 and 121)

Pl. X

Smiling terracotta Yaksha in the round from Pitalkhora caves, Maharashtra, c. 50 B.C. (*see* p. 117)

Pl. XI

Female figure in ivory from Ter, District Osmananabad, Maharashtra, c. 100 A.D. (*see* p. 120)

Pl. XII

(a) (*Left*) Smiling boy from Nevasa, c. 100 A.D.
(*Right*) half of a female figure in terracotta from
Tamluk, District Midnapur, West Bengal. (*see*
pp. 106 and 120).

(b) Terracotta figure of woman showing pleated blo-
use and skirt and *odhani*
from Badopal, now in the
Bikaner Museum, c. 200
A.D. (*see* pp. 106 and 120)

pottery, or of chipping, polishing and grinding of stone implements which characterize the Chalcolithic and Neolithic cultures. It is possible, as argued by some anthropologists, that this is due to de-socializing and de-culturalizing factors. For example within historic times some of the tribes like the Hunas and Gurjaras, having once been empire-builders, have sunk back to a life of shepherds. This is possible. But the links with the past have to be established. These might be had if excavations in the present secluded habitat of the primitive tribes are carried out and yield traces of cultures which they (their ancestors) had carried with them when pushed back by the oncoming Aryans.

There is also another way or possibility of identifying the bearers of the Chalcolithic Cultures. It has already been argued from the juxtaposition of Mahabharata sites and Grey Ware sites in the Ganga-Yamuna Doab, by Shri Lal[193] that the Grey Ware people might be a group of Aryans or the Mahabharata people, whereas the probability of the Malwa or Maheshwar-Navdatoli people, as Haihayas or a mixed Aryan tribe from Iran, has also been pointed out by the writer.[194] Likewise, the various pottery cultures in Southern Rajputana and Saurashtra might be attributed to the various Yadava tribes. In the same way we may account for the Deccan Chalcolithic as the result of the southward migration of one of the Aryan tribes.[195]

With some plausibility, then, we may attribute the Chalcolithic Cultures of the Chambal, Narmada, Tapi-Godavari Valleys to some of the Aryan tribes. All these are tied by common features and differ from valley to valley according to the pottery fabrics and types. But their basic way of life remains the same.

This theory would remain unconfirmed unless and until some writing is found in their excavated habitations which identifies at least some of them with one or two of the Puranic or Vedic tribes. But this may never be found, as they were illiterate—and

[193] In *A.I.* Nos. 10-11, p. 151.

[194] In *Illustrated London News,* September 5, 1959 and *Sārdha-Satābdī special volume* published by the Asiatic Society of Bombay (New Series), 1959, pp. 229-39.

[195] Cf. also, Allchin (*op. cit.,* p. 140-41), who on very slender evidence attributes the birth of the Deccan Neolithic culture to a Dravidoid or Indo-European stock from Iran and Central Asia, thus ruling out its indigenous origin.

Aryans are believed to have been illiterate—in spite of the high philosophical and spiritual content of the Rigvedic *mantras,* in spite of the metaphysical speculations of the Upanishads, and in spite of the earliest etymological efforts of Yaska and the first systematic grammar of Sanskrit by Panini.

Thus, the actors on the Chalcolithic stage remain hazy, almost unknown. It is towards their identity that all our efforts should now be directed.

This uncertainty about the identity of the Chalcolithic people does not enable us to accept wholly the view that the impetus to march forward from the Stone Age—from the stage of a savage and barbarian—came from Western Asia, particularly the grassy hill country of "the Fertile Crescent" (of Braidwood and Breasted) which is regarded as the cradle of civilization.[196] Professor Braidwood himself has recently made a significant statement while "seeking the world's first farmers in Persian Kurdistan."[197] He says, "It continues to appear that the more important generative factors in the appearance of effective plant and animal domestication are not to be sought in the facile explanations of environmental determinism." Striking also are the words, "Since this zone (of grassy and open oakland) runs from Shiraz in Iran through highland Iraq and the southern flanks of Turkey to southern Syria—a distance of some 1,200 miles—we do not suppose that either our previous Iraq sites (e.g., Karim Shahir, Jarmo) or our sites near Kermansha are in any way unique instances either in time or place wherein food production began. Our sites simply happen to be those which the accident of archaeological discovery has allowed us to examine so far."

Thus, on the one hand, the view about one or two regions alone being the birth place of civilization is being revised. On the other, if it is proved by further work that some of the primitive or aboriginal tribes are to be credited with the Mesolithic

[196] Braidwood, Robert J., and Howe, Bruce, *Prehistoric Investigations in Iruqui Kurdistan,* Chicago, 1960. p. 11.

[197] *Illustrated London News,* October 22, 1960, pp. 695-97. Sir Mortimer Wheeler (*Early India and Pakistan,* p. 148) attributes the origin of the Chalcolithic cultures to the microlithic cultures. This seems to be wrong, as it does not take into consideration the difference between the microliths and the stone blade industries of the later period.

and even the Chalcolithic cultures as even Sir Mortimer Wheeler seems to think, then naturally, it would imply that these are indigenous or autochthon and not inspired by outside influences. Then the relation of this fact to the geographic factors will have to be re-examined. Otherwise, on the current theory, it is held that the bearers of a superior culture came along the principal lines of communication and gradually occupied the most fertile river valleys, ousting the hunters and food-gatherers to Central Indian forests and hills. It is in this way that we can explain the unequal development of Indian civilization: for some areas, because of their natural resources and nearness to the highways, attracted settlers; some, like Northern Gujarat, because of semi-aridity were settled late, and others, like Assam, Kerala and Central Indian forests, became refugee areas—areas of isolation—where the aboriginal tribes continued to live on in a hunting stage until today.[198]

[198] See Subbarao, B., *The Personality of India,* pp. 20-27 and Fig. 6, 2nd Edition, Baroda 1958.

# III

# INDIAN ARCHAEOLOGY AND ITS CONTRIBUTION TO PROTOHISTORY AND EARLY HISTORY

In the last lecture, I have dealt at length with all the aspects of prehistory and also certain aspects of protohistory. In particular I explained the significance of the new discoveries in the Gangetic Valley, Central India and the Deccan and the light these throw on the Aryan problem. There are, however, one or two other aspects of protohistory which have got to be mentioned now, before I pass on to ancient Indian history. This is the subject of megaliths or megalithic monuments.

Megaliths (from the Greek: *megas* great and *lithos* stone) are a particular kind of monuments erected usually, but not necessarily, with huge, rough undressed stones. They have been known since the last century, particularly by the works of Meadows Taylor, James Fergusson, Jagor, Rea, Louis Lapique, Breeks and others.[1] Since many of these monuments were found in several districts of South India, including the former Hyderabad State, it was only in this region that they had received some attention. But unfortunately none of the monuments was systematically excavated. In fact at some sites these megaliths were blasted by dynamite and so the cultural significance of these monuments was completely lost, and people went on using names like "Dolmen", "Cromlechs", "Stone Circles", etc. It was however left to Sir Mortimer Wheeler[2] and anthropologists like Professors Hutton and Haimendorf to tell us that there were at least two kinds of megaliths in India. In the South they belonged to a past period and were mainly tombs, whereas in the East—Assam, Bihar and parts of Orissa—they were primarily memorials to the dead and represented a living tradition (as these are still being made by some primitive tribes[3]). This also seems to be the

[1] For detailed information, see *A.I.*, No. 9, 1953, p. 103, ff.

[2] Wheeler, R.E.M., *A.I.* No. 4, 1947, pp. 147-310.

[3] For instance the Khasis of Assam, see Gurdon, P.R.T., *The Khasis*, London, 1914, p. 145; and for Bihar, the brief article by Adris Banerji "Bihar Megaliths, etc." in *Indian Historical Quarterly*, Vol. XXXVI, 1960, pp. 13-16.

case near Poona where small megalithic monuments were discovered by the writer as far back as 1939.[4] Here too, they are not burials or tombs, but merely memorials to the dead. Unfortunately the Eastern megaliths have not been fully surveyed. But the work in South India has begun and we now know the exact significance of these monuments, the main types, the method of construction and their probable age.[5] In his usually methodical manner, Wheeler set one person first to prepare a list of types of these monuments, whereas he himself very carefully excavated these monuments at Brahmagiri in the District of Chitaldrug in Mysore State. Since then explorations[6] are being conducted every year in the Madras, Mysore and Andhra States and many sites have brought to light several types of megaliths, whereas Srinivasan[7] has very well summarized the evidence from early Tamil-Sangam-literature and inscriptions about the various methods of disposing of the dead. Three out of the four methods would fall into some of the types mentioned below.

To date, Krishnaswami classifies the megaliths into the following types:[8] Dolmenoid Cist and Cairn Circle (Chingleput area) with two or more sub-types; Cairn and Cist (former Pudokottai State); Multiple Dolmens, Port-hole Cist, Menhirs, Umbrella stones, Hood stones and Rock-cut caves (former Cochin State). According to the geological and physiographic features, the first are confined to the eastern mountains, the second to the laterite plains and the third to the coastal strip.

This list, of course, will have to be revised as every year more and more sub-types[9] are being found, owing to intensive explora-

[4] Sankalia, H.D., "Megalithic Monuments near Poona", *Bulletin, Deccan College Research Institute,* Vol. I, 1939-40, pp. 178-84.

[5] Wheeler, *op.cit.;* Thapar, B.K., *A.I.,* No. 8, 1952, pp. 3-16. Banerjee, N.R., *A.I.,* No. 12, 1956, pp. 21-34; Thapar, B.K., *A.I.,* No. 13, 1957, pp. 26-37; Banerjee, N.R. and Soundara Rajan, K.V., *A.I.,* No. 15, 1959, pp. 4-42.

[6] *I.A.R.,* 1955-56, p. 23; 1956-57, p. 31 and 34-36; 1957-58, p. 38; 1958-59, pp. 6, 32; 1959-60, pp. 6-9, 37.

[7] Srinivasan, K.R., "The Megalithic Burials and Urn Fields of South India in the Light of Tamil Literature and Tradition", *A.I.,* No. 2, 1946, pp. 9-16.

[8] Krishnaswami, V.D., *A.I.,* No. 5, 1949, pp. 35-45.

[9] For instance at Kunnattur, Chingleput District, where in 1955-56 and
(*Contd. on p.* 102)

tion in South India. Wheeler's excavation and later work in the Chingleput District of Madras State and elsewhere definitely tell us that these monuments are not very old. However, the view that they are not older than 4th century B.C. has also got to be revised in view of the fact that iron objects and Black-and-Red pottery has since been found in North India in an earlier context. Of course it remains true that these monuments herald the Iron Age in South India. It is, however, important to remember that these monuments, though every one of them is some kind of a tomb, are not primary burials. Almost all are secondary burials; that is, the body or bodies after death were left exposed to beasts and weather and it was only later that the remains that were left were collected together and buried in a pot (called urn) or a chest-like stone (rectangular cist) but if above ground and in the shape of a table with one huge capstone covering the three or more upright stones it was called a "dolmen" or "dolmenoid cist," or a legged, oblong vessel with a separate lid and legs (called sarcophagus) along with the most important possessions of the dead—iron weapons and tools, shell ornaments, semi-precious beads, pots of various shapes and even horse-bits and occasionally coins. The view that the bodies of the dead were previously "macerated"[10] in pits surrounded by stone circles is also not confirmed by excavations at Nagarjunakonda.[11] In fact here two pits contained fully articulated skeletons which indicate that we may expect in some megaliths complete burials, and not necessarily collections of bones gathered at a subsequent date.

The fact that pits were prepared for the secondary burials and then enclosed by large slabs of stones and the whole finally surrounded by a circle of stones implies a fairly well established and prosperous social organization. It has been observed[12] that these megalith builders of South India, while they chose high, rocky ground for the burials owing to the proximity of the raw material

1956-57 and at Jadiyenahalli, Bangalore, variations from the usual types were observed.

[10] That is, the place where bodies were exposed and later a few selected bones picked up and interred in a cist grave called "inverted towers of silence" by Wheeler.

[11] *I.A.R.*, 1959-60, pp. 2 and 9 respectively.

[12] Srinivasan, K.R., and Banerjee, N.R. in *A.I.*, No. 9, p. 109 and Banerjee, N.R. in *A.I.*, No. 12, 1956, p. 23.

—laterite blocks or granite or underground caves in Kerala—had also dug irrigation tanks in the flat alluvial plains indicating thereby that they were not only a settled people, but very intelligent agriculturists.[13] Though we have no idea of their villages or towns, as none of their habitations has been even partially excavated, some idea of their life can be gathered from the earliest Tamil, known popularly as *Sangam* literature. But the question that is vexing the minds of scholars—anthropologists, archaeologists and others—is the identity of these first rice-eaters of South India (as yet no evidence of these grains is available from this part of India, though rice has been found at Kolhapur in second century A.D. houses, and in Central India as early as the 12th century B.C., besides Hastinapur where it can be dated to at least the 8-9th century B.C.). Skeletal remains—including skulls—are of little help as these are often disarticulated and in a fragmentary condition. Zuckerman[14] believed from a study of Adichallanur skulls that the people were Dravidians (that is the skulls, etc. showed similarity to those of the present day speakers of the Dravidian tongues). Christoph von Fürer-Haimendorf, a cultural anthropologist, propounded a very interesting theory of far reaching importance. He suggested that the megalith-builders were a people of Mediterranean stock who probably came to the West Coast by sea, entered South India in about 500 B.C. and spread northwards subduing the earlier neolithic and microlithic people who were in a semi-nomadic, food-gathering stage of culture. Further, since the distribution of South Indian megaliths was almost coterminus with that of the Dravidian languages, it is this people who should have introduced the Dravidian language (or languages) in the region. And it is their kings—the Cholas, Cheras and Pandyas—to whom the Asokan edicts were addressed. Thus, the earliest Tamil should go back to about 500 B.C.

The basic evidence on which Haimendorf relied for propounding

13 At Maski, however, Thapar noticed burials in the habitation area itself and a north-south orientation instead of the east-west, as well as a few other features. See Thapar, B.K., *A.I.*, No. 13, 1957, p. 27. Perhaps this is a legacy or influence due to inhabiting an earlier Chalcolithic site.

14 Zuckerman, S., "The Adichanallur Skulls," *Bulletin Madras Government Museum*, N.S., General Section, Pt. II, 1930, pp. 19-20.

his theory was that a certain group of megaliths known as dol-menoid cist with port-hole occurred in Western European mega-liths. The latter, however, are not later than 2000 B.C. and do not contain any iron objects. Thus chronologically and in one of the important cultural aspects, these European megaliths are far removed, geographically and in time, from the South Indian mega-liths. The structural affinity between both thus remains unexplained.

Moreover speculations about the Dravidian or proto-Dravidian also remains uncorroborated, because, as the late Professor Gordon Childe told us in a personal discussion, we have very few indications of Dravidian languages in Western Europe, except, of course, Finnish-Ugrian, which some people believe contains elements of the Dravidian language. However, the case is quite different from that of the Sanskrit and Indo-European. Here there is no doubt that Sanskrit and Iranian are intimately connected with several European languages. Unless, therefore, we find proto-Dravidian languages in Western Europe, it will be very difficult to accept a theory of such far-fetched significance and to suggest that the megalith-builders introduced the Dravidian tongue into South India. There is another aspect as well, which was, of course, not known to Professor Haimendorf as no work of this nature had been done. The practice of burying the dead in pits or pots has been found to be associated with all Chalcolithic cultures of the Deccan and Peninsular India. Recent small ex-cavations at T. Narsipur in Mysore and Nagarjunakonda and Piklihal in Andhra have also shown that the earlier Neolithic people were probably not so nomadic but could boast of a settled life in which, besides polished stones axes, spouted and other pots played an important part and the people had some idea of life after death.

The megalith builders improved upon this state of culture by introducing iron and irrigation (?), but this improvement was certainly not so much as previously thought. Some of the burial practices—such as the use of lime and urns—they might have adopted from their predecessors. It is further possible that these Neolithic people as well as some of the Chalcolithic people from the north were proto- (or better pre-) Dravidian.[14a] The whole

14a See also Allchin above footnote 191a.

problem is at a very interesting stage and unless anthropologists, linguisticians, and archaeologists come forward no proper solution of this question can be had in the foreseeable future.

## ANCIENT HISTORY

The chief feature of ancient history now is that coins and inscriptions are not our only source of dating the various historical periods—a thing which characterized our reconstruction of history for nearly the last 100 years. Two new things have been introduced by archaeology. One is pottery, the significance of which I have already discussed in the first lecture.

To this I would here add a few words about Rangmahal pottery and the contribution of its culture to that of Rajputana.

Rangmahal[15] is one of the centrally situated sites on the dry bed of the Ghaggar (the ancient Sarasvati) in the northern part of the former Bikaner State. The region is now almost a desert. It was explored by Shri A. Ghosh, the present Director-General of Archaeology in India during the years 1950-53, when over 200 mounds were examined. Those at Rangmahal and others gave a very distinctive type of pottery. This is beautifully dark-red and extremely well baked. The surfaces are painted with black designs. There are a large number of shapes, including the famous sprinklers in Red Polished Ware but the most striking are vessels with flattish and highly carinated neck and shoulders with a razor-like sharp edge. These are often painted, but at times decorated with incised or stamped designs.[16]

The beautiful fabrics and decoration reminded one of the similar well-made Harappa pottery. It could be thought that Rangmahal, though a new culture, was possibly an immediate descendant of the Harappa Civilization.

However, when the site was excavated by Hanna Rydh in 1952-54, it was found that it was not older than the 2nd-3rd century A.D.[17] though it was still maintained that the Rangmahal pottery somehow continued the Harappa tradition. This may be. What is important to remember is the influence of this culture

---

[15] Hanna Rydh, *Rang Mahal,* Lund, Sweden, 1959, p. 43.
[16] *Ibid.,* Fig. 102, p. 141 and others.
[17] *Ibid.,* p. 181.

on the subsequent culture of Rajputana.

The coins found at Rangmahal suggest that it was settled during the Kushana rule. However, from the distribution of the Rangmahal pottery and its variants, it may be said that the culture had spread as far south as Saurashtra and Northern and Central Gujarat.[18] This may be attributed to the Saka Satraps, who are believed to be the viceroys of the Kushanas. We may therefore call it a Saka-Kushana pottery.

Now on the one hand, this Rangmahal pottery seems to be connected with the Cemetery H pottery from Harappa of which two sites had been noted in Bahawalpur, on the other with the pottery still current in Rajputana (including Bikaner and Jodhpur). However, of signal significance are terracotta figures[19] found at Badopal, Rangmahal, etc., and now exhibited in the Bikaner Museum. In these, the women are shown with a large pleated skirt and sari covering their head, but keeping a part of the skirt uncovered, and a pleated bodice, with some applique kind of work done on the portion covering the breast.[20] In another, the *odhani* falls down on the either side of the body, and the breast seems to be uncovered, whereas a full, pleated skirt goes up to the ankle. (Pl. XII b)

This was exactly the dress of women in Rajputana, Central India and Saurashtra, until very recently, and is still being worn by the Lamana women (a gypsy type of people) even outside these regions.

Now this kind of skirt and short sari, called the *Langha* and *Odhani* respectively and bodice are quite different[21] from the dress depicted in earlier and later Indian sculptures. Usually there

[18] And should be found in Western Malwa, particularly at Ujjain, which was the capital of the Saka (Kardamaka family) for nearly 200 years.

[19] Agrawala, R. C., in *Artibus Asiae*, Vol. XIX, 1956, p. 61, fig. 2. These were first discovered by Dr. L. P. Tessitori. See *Archaeological Survey of India Annual Report*, 1917-18, Part I.

[20] This is exactly like the manner of dressing found among the Minas— an ancient tribe of north-eastern Bikaner and Saurashtra tribes. A model of the former is shown in the museum at Jaipur.

[21] This was noticed previously by Goetz H., *Art and Architecture of Bikaner State*, Oxford, 1950, p. 26, and regarded as Hellenistic, whereas Agrawala, (*op.cit.*, p. 63) seems to miss the significance, though according to him Dr. Motichandra (*Pracina Bharatiya Vesabhusa*, p. 125) had already noticed their first association with the Kushanas.

was no skirt and the sari was worn between the legs and not round them.

Thus, we may credit the authors of the Rangmahal culture—whether they be Sakas, Kushanas, Palhavas or somebody else—with many distinctive features of Rajputana culture.

The second new thing introduced by archaeology is carbon-14 method of dating. This is useful not only for dating the prehistoric or protohistoric cultures, but it is equally useful for dating the historical periods as well. For instance, the *Bajri* (a kind of millet) grains which were found in a well at Nevasa have been dated to about 1,800 years before the present time by carbon-14 method. Now this dating tallies very well with what we know of this period from the coins as well as other antiquities found at Nevasa, and if in future many more objects from different sites can be so dated, then the value of coins will not decrease, but will get additional confirmation.

The third most important feature of the work during the last 20 years is that a number of sites all over India—in the south, in the east, in the north as well as western India and central India have been excavated, which enables us to know the life in the ancient past—a fact which we do not know very well except for the political or dynastic histories, and some idea of the art and architecture. I will refer to a few aspects in this lecture. For instance, excavations at Taxila undertaken by Sir John Marshall and carried on for a number of years have now been published in three magnificent volumes[22], and from them we know that Taxila was a well laid out city in about the 2nd century A.D. and that this city owed its particular feature of planning to the Indo-Greeks. The same features can be found at Charsada near Peshawar, which has been excavated by Sir Mortimer Wheeler in 1959.[23] Then our small excavations at Kolhapur in 1945-46[24] as well as those at Sisupalgarh tell us that between two houses there was a small passage of 2 feet or so. These houses, whether in Taxila, Sisupalgarh, Arikemedu, Nevasa or Nasik, were provided with a kind of sanitary arrangement, which has since then

22 Marshall, Sir John, *Taxila,* 1951.
23 See, *Illustrated London News,* February 7, 1959, pp. 232-35.
24 Sankalia, H.D. and Dikshit, M.G., *Excavations at Kolhapur,* Poona. 1952.

been lost. Every house has a ring-well or a brick-well into which all the dirty (?) things were cast. And so we find in the excavation reports illustrations of these 'soak pits' as they are called. Even now such soak pits are in use in Karnatak and in Central India.

Secondly, we know from Sisupalgarh as well as Ujjain and Kausambi that these cities were very well fortified. A huge mud rampart provided with gates went round the entire city or the important buildings in which probably the king or the minister lived.[25] The houses were roofed with a very fine kind of tile, a contrivance which has disappeared from India in recent times. These houses were further provided with landings and stair-cases, which can compare very well with some of the easy stairs we find in modern buildings. I shall give only two examples—one from Sisupalgarh and the other from Nagarjunakonda. At the latter place, we have got, I think, the first *ghat* going back to about the 2nd-3rd century A.D. However, what I have described here is almost insignificant,[26] because except Nagarjunakonda, no site is fully excavated and we do not know the plans of the towns, cities or villages in any period of our ancient history. Barring Taxila, we have no plan of any Gupta, Chalukya or a Pallava city, and therefore, we do not know how the ordinary people or the kings lived. What we know today is only something about their political history and a little of the art of the period. This is indeed insufficient to have an idea of the past and, therefore, what we need is horizontal excavations at select places in different parts of India.

## EPIGRAPHY

From this let us pass on to the other normal sources of ancient history, and I will only briefly indicate here the salient features

[25] Very recently, this season, Professor G. R. Sharma has unearthed a fine stone structure in pre-Northern Black Polished Pottery deposits at Kausambi. He thinks that this might be the palace of king Udayana, about 6th century B.C. I am profoundly thankful to Prof. Sharma for permitting me to cite the latest results of his excavation.

[26] For other aspects of houses and references, see Sankalia, H.D. "Houses and Habitations through the Ages", *Bulletin of the Deccan College Research Institute,* Vol. 20, pp. 140-63.

of the contributions made by epigraphy, numismatics, etc. unravelling our ancient past. I have made no attempt to give you a complete bibliography in any of these subjects, because this can now be found in the excellent bibliography which is being prepared by the Kern Institute from Leyden in Holland,[27] or in the short survey published in *Ancient India*[28] and *Indian Archaeology—A Review*.[29] Two other attempts should also be mentioned. One is the bibliography published by Professor Moraes[30] and the other by Sibsen Chaudhary.

Interest in epigraphy has certainly decreased during the last 20 years. There are very few scholars who can read the ancient Brahmi script. The reasons are twofold. Possibly epigraphy is a difficult subject, and so people are not interested in it. Secondly, scholars as well as students do not get an opportunity to decipher inscriptions. The one result is that unlike the earlier volumes of the *Epigraphia Indica,* the recent volumes of this journal published by the Government of India are dominated by one person, viz., the Editor. It was formerly the practice of the Department of Epigraphy to send out inscriptions to other scholars in different parts of India and even outside. This has now been stopped and the result is that the interest in the subject is fast decreasing, and I am afraid that if this policy persists then within 10 years there will be no scholars in India, except a few who work at Ootacamund, who will know anything of epigraphy.

Coming now to the important discoveries, I shall only refer here to what I think is important for the cultural history of India, because there are a number of inscriptions which deal with history of the various dynasties. But none of these, as far as I can say, have in any way revolutionised what we know of Indian history. And, therefore, I am not giving you something like a bibliographical list of these publications. But one thing that is remarkable is the discovery of Asokan edicts at Kandahar in Afghanistan. Here, just on the very outskirts of the city near the hills which

27 *Annual Bibliography of Indian Archaeology,* Vol. XV, 1940-47, Vol. XVI, 1948-53, published in 1950 and 1958, respectively.

28 "Ten Years of Indian Epigraphy", in *A.I.,* No. 5, pp. 46-61.

29 This gives a brief account of the latest discoveries from year to year.

30 Moraeas, George M., *Bibliography of Indological Studies,* 1942 and 1943, published in 1945 and 1952, respectively.

protect Kandahar from the west, Asokan edicts were discovered in 1958, by the French[31] and Italian[32] Missions; whether the discovery was independently or jointly made is not clear. The inscription is bilingual; i.e. there are two languages in which it is written, one is Greek and the other is Aramaic. This is not the first time that an inscription in Greek is found in Afghanistan, but it is the oldest. Of course, Aramaic was used in North-West India. It was the court language of the Achaemenian emperors of Iran and, therefore, it is no wonder that this language should be used for the inscription. Greek should also have been there. But unfortunately so far nothing was found in Greek at so early a period. From the point of view of Asoka's teachings, it means that he not only preached to the kingdoms on his frontier, but he went out of his way in preaching to them in languages which were well known to them. This is the first large Aramaic inscription; otherwise only small bits were known from the Punjab. The inscription is also important from the point of view of its contents. Unlike other inscriptions it mentions that owing to the efforts of Asoka, there is joy in the world, there is less suffering, there is less of uncleanliness and this is due to a number of reasons mentioned in the edicts. And a concrete instance is cited saying that even it has been prohibited to catch fish—an injunction which has not been found in other edicts of Asoka.

Another copy of Asoka's Minor Rock Edict I was found in 1953 at Gujarra in the Datia District, Vindhya Pradesh, about 12 miles to the north of Jhansi.[33] This is the second set of edicts where Asoka is mentioned by his name 'Asokaraja'. So far this important feature was noticed in the edict at Maski in the Raichur District. Thus, there is no doubt that the author of the edicts was Asoka and nobody else as some people tried to make out, some 15 years ago. I hope you know that an attempt was made to show that Samprati, the grandson of Asoka[34] got the edicts engraved. The third place where Asokan edicts have been

[31] In *Journal Asiatique*, Tome CCXLVI, 1958, pp. 1-48.

[32] In *East and West*, Vol. 9, 1958, pp. 192 ff and Vol. 10, 1959, pp. 243 ff. The inscription is here reproduced with the courtesy of Dr. Tucci who also readily supplied the photographs.

[33] *Epigraphia Indica*, Vol. XXXI, pp. 205-10.

[34] Shah, Tribhuvandas, *Ancient India*, in 4 vols.

found is Erragudi in the Kurnool District.[35]  Of course, these were
known as far back as 1928, but it is only during the last 10 years
that these edicts have seen the light of day. Sopara, near Bombay
where in 1882 an Asokan edict had been found, has recently
yielded a fragment of Edict IX.[36]  This means that all the 14
edicts must have been originally engraved somewhere in the vicinity of Sopara.  A vigorous search is necessary to discover them.

Of signal importance is a small inscription excavated at
Kausambi, near Allahabad.  It gives the name of the building as
Goshitarama.  Now we know from Hiuen Tsang and early Pali
literature that the Buddha had visited the place.  Though the
record is not of the Buddha period, it no doubt suggests that the
earliest building at that particular place in Kausambi, near the
rampart, might go back to the time of the Buddha. Thus this
would be the earliest dated (indirectly) building in India.

In this context I would like to cite the stupa unearthed by
the late Dr. Altekar at Vaisāli,[37] in Bihar.  No inscription is associated with it, but from the nature of the pottery found in its core,
it is argued that this is the earliest Buddhist stupa in India, containing the ashes of the Buddha, which was later enlarged twice or
thrice.

While the discovery of these edicts enlarges the extent of the
spread of Asoka's teachings, a Brahmi inscription[38] in a cave at
Mamandur, near Kanchi (Conjeeveram) in North Arcot District
seems to be written in early Tamil language.  This along with
the graffiti from Arikamedu[39] will prove useful in reconstructing
the history of this language.  The short Arikamedu inscriptions
are in the ancient Dravidi script[40] which is allied to Brahmi.  If
this is so, what was the script of the Dravidians who are supposed
to be late arrivals in South India?

We have all read of the revival of Vedic religion in about the
1st century B.C.-A.D.  Till now the best evidence for this was

---

[35] *Epigraphia Indica*, Vol. XXXII, pp. 1-28.  A Minor Edict, similar to
that as Erragudi has recently been found at Rajula-Mandagiri in the same
district, *I.A.R.*, 1953-54, p. 13.

[36] *Ibid.*, pp. 29-30.

[37] *I.A.R.*, 1957-58, pp. 10-11.

[38] *A.I.*, No. 5, p. 51.

[39] *Ibid.*, No. 2, pp. 109-114.

[40] *Ibid.*, No. 5, p. 57.

supplied by inscriptions of the Satavahana dynasty at Nanaghat, near Junnar, Poona District. These referred to the performance of a number of Vedic sacrifices and the donation of thousands of cows and other things to Brahmanas. These, however, seemed to be a solitary example. Corroboration of similar practices from other parts of India was badly required. This is now supplied by a group of *yupa* inscriptions[41] from south-east Rajputana, and the discovery of the ruins of an *asvamedha* sacrifice site, together with an inscription of one king Silavarman, at Jagatram, District Dehra Dun. The inscription is of about the 3rd-4th century, to judge from its script, and specifically refers to the performance of the *asvamedha* sacrifice at the spot.[42]

A *yupa* originally was a sacrificial pillar of wood, round which the man or animal to be immolated was tied. Vedic texts like the *Aitareya* and *Satapatha Brahmana* have laid down the specifications about the size and shape of the pillar and praised the virtues of such a perfect *yupa*.

Now the several *yupas* that have been discovered at Isapur, Nandsa, Badva, etc. in Eastern Rajputana are all of stone; so also are the *yupas* in far off Borneo, erected by king Mulavarman. The Indian stone *yupas* try to conform to the shapes, etc. laid down by the *Brahmanas,* but in one very important particular they depart from the Vedic injunctions which were emphasized by the writers of the *Srauta* and *Dharmasutras* like Vasistha, Baudhayana, Visnu. These 5th-6th century B.C. authors had proscribed the use of stone *yupas*—as something unclean. Nevertheless, we find these injunctions flouted by the kings, generals and others of the 2nd-4th century A.D. Numerous *yupas* had been erected in the land, doubtless, as sacrificial memorials. Indeed, the performance of *asvamedha* and other sacrifices and the erection of *yupas* as a necessary consequence thereof had imparted to the *yupas* the significance of a *jayastambha* (pillar of victory), as pointed out by Dr. Altekar. Hence Kalidasa extolled the planting of *yupas* by king Kartavirya all over the land (literally 18 continents—*dvipas*).

41 See Altekar, A.S., in *Epigraphia Indica,* Vol. XXIII, pp. 42-52 and earlier references cited therein; and also Chhabra, B.Ch., "Yupa Inscriptions" in *India Antiqua,* Kern Institute, Leyden, 1947, pp. 77-82.
42 *I.A.R.,* 1953-54, p. 10, pl. XIII-XIV.

The *yupa* inscriptions from Badva commemorate the performance of a Trirātra sacrifice. This has been described in detail in the *Taittiriya-Samhita*. By its performance the sacrificer can win for himself whatever is three-fold in wordly as well as spiritual affairs. The sacrifice was to be performed for three days, and every day 333 cows were to be given as *dakshina*.

There are many other details which had to be scrupulously observed. But suffice it to say that these rituals gave a fresh lease of life to the ancient Vedic religion for several centuries, until it was gradually given up because of the rising tide of the cult of *bhakti* (or devotion to a personal god).

Another important feature which characterizes these *yupa* records is that almost all are dated in an era which is called *Krita*. Though the exact significance of this expression is not known yet, in about the 4th century it was ~placed by the term "Malava", which in its turn was called "Vikram " only in the 11th century. Thus the present Vikrama era which is urrent in Gujarat, Rajputana and Uttar Pradesh is over 2,000 years old, but its *name* not more than a thousand! People forgot its antecedents and ascribed its foundation to a king Vikrama who no doubt had ruled over the Malavas, and probably adopted the era current amongst them. The *yupa* inscriptions, thus, give the "prehistory" of the Vikrama era.

The occurrence of *yupas* in far off Borneo has already been referred to. This fact alone vouches for the resurgence and rapid spread of the Vedic religion. Otherwise, how can one account for the *yupas* in such distant islands considering the slow modes of travel in those times?

Another interesting epigraphical discovery is from Sonda[43], Sirsi Taluka, North Kanara District, now in Mysore. We have records of kings and others who performed sacrifices, but here is a unique instance of a 'sacrificial memorial'. For while the inscription refers to the performance of a *soma-yaga* (sacrifice) by one Sarvajna-sarasvati, a pontiff (priest) of Homnehalli under the guidance of a Srauti Visvapatibhatta who was specially invited from Kasi, at the same time a tablet was set up on the sacrificial spot. On it are engraved the *Vedi* (the raised seat for the per-

[43] Desai, P.B., "Sacrificial Inscription from Sonda", *Epigraphia Indica*, Vol. XXXII, p. 79.

former), in the centre, whereas to its south, east and north are depicted three pits for the three sacred fires known as *Garhapatya, Daksina* and *Ahavaniya.*

When the old rituals and sacrifices are being fast forgotten, this 17th century (1674 A.D.) inscription and sacrificial memorial should serve as a fitting testimony to our past cultural history.

Extremely interesting for the political, social and religious history of Western India, in particular the present Thana District, are the sets of copper plate inscriptions[44] from Chinchani in the Dahnu Taluka. These were discovered only a few years ago, in 1955, and belong to the period when the Rashtrakutas and their vassals, the Śilāharas, were ruling in Maharashtra, in the 10th century A.D. It was known from the account of Muslim merchants and historians—Sulaiman (851 A.D.), Abu Zaid, Ibn Khurdadba (912 A.D.), Al Ma'sudi (932-33 A.D.) and others —that the Rastrakutas treated the Arab Muslims well, unlike the contemporary Gurjara kings of Rajputana and Kanauj. But it was never realized—in fact it comes as a great surprise to us all—that a Muslim ruler named Madhumati or Sugatipa belonging to the Tajika (Arab) community was appointed as a governor of the district (*mandala*) of Sanjan, by the Rastrakuta emperor Krishna II (878-915 A.D.) and that he remained in this position under Krishna's successor, Indra III (915-928 A.D.). As in the earlier period, the Arab names are Sanskritized. Madhumati is undoubtedly Muhammad, but others are not so easy to explain. This also confirms the statement of Ibn Haukal and Al Istakhri that none but the Muslims ruled over their co-religionists in the Rastrakuta domain, implying thereby, as Dr. Sircar says[45], that the *Qazis* decided the religious and judicial affairs of the Arab Muslims, just as nearly 1,000 years later an Englishman could claim European jurors in an Indian court.

Later on it appears that the Silaharas regained control of the whole of the Konkan. But soon their hold over Thana became weak, for a Modha, named Vijjala, from Southern Rajputana is found in charge of the Sanjan Mandala in 1048 A.D.[46] Modhas, as is well known, form an important sub-caste among Gujarati

44 *Epigraphia Indica,* Vol. XXXII, 1959, pp. 45-60.
45 *Ibid.,* p. 50.
46 *Ibid.,* pp. 63-76.

Baniyas. They, like the Porvads, hail originally from Rajputana and occupy important positions today in industry and commerce in Bombay. This is, however, the earliest reference to their entry into (Greater) Bombay.

These Modhas had also brought their gods and goddesses with them and built temples.

Sanjan and Thana had members of other communities[47] from other provinces as well, such as Tamil, Telugu, Sarasvatas and Bengalis (Gaudiya), besides the Parsees, who are specifically mentioned as *hamyamana paura* (citizens of *hamyamana*). It is not Sanjan which is separately mentioned, but probably it is derived from Avestic *hanjamana* and Persian *anjuman*. So Sanjan was primarily a Parsee colony. It held the same place in the 10th century in Western India, as I have said elsewhere[48], which Bombay holds today.

While all these were outsiders, the original, local, population (aboriginals) consisted of Kolis and Maharas; hence the small territorial units—*visayas*—are named after them. It is for the first time that we hear of these communities in this region. Thus these incidental inscriptional references are important for tracing the early history of the aboriginal tribes in Western India.

### NUMISMATICS

Few sensational discoveries have been made in numismatics in the last 20 years. Off and on we hear of hoards of punch-marked coins and others like those of the Satavahanas, Guptas, etc. The hoards of the punch-marked coins add little to our knowledge about their chronology or distribution. A small collection of surface copper-punch-marked coins from Nagari[49] is interesting, because the coins are in different denominations and these denominations also correspond to the number of symbols. Thus the larger coins have got five and three symbols respectively, whereas the smaller coins have got one symbol only. This is the first

---

[47] See, *Ibid.*, particularly p. 64, which refers to the elders of the Parsee community and so many other local and district officers and others—all of which cannot be mentioned here.

[48] *Journal, Gujarat Research Society,* Vol. XXII, 1960, p. 325.

[49] *Journal of the Numismatic Society of India,* Vol. XVII, 1955, pp. 1-28.

time that such a relation can be observed between the different denominations of punch-marked coins. But the most important, as far as the various coin types of the Gupta period are concerned, is a hoard from Bayana in the former Bharatpur State. This has been fully worked out by the late Dr. Altekar[50] and the report on it has also been published. He has followed this up by preparing an up-to-date account of the *Coinage of the Gupta Empire*.[51] Similarly the Tarhala hoard of Andhra coins has been described by Dr. Mirashi.[52] Shri Singhal[53] has given us a bibliography of works published till 1950 and Dr. Gupta has prepared a detailed monograph on punch-marked coins. However, none of these collections have solved any important problem in the dynastic history of India. This can happen, I think, only when more and more coins are found in stratified excavations as at Nevasa.[54] Unfortunately our collection is neither large nor are many coins readable. But if in future many more coins are found, then we shall be able to reconstruct the Satavahana chronology more accurately than at present.

## ARCHITECTURE

Very few monuments—caves, temples, stupas, etc.—have been found which could throw light on the development of these monuments in India. However, every year discoveries are being made which add to our knowledge of their distribution and occurrence in different parts of India. For instance, the very recent discovery of a Buddhist stupa and monastery of the 4th-5th century A.D. (with figures of Buddha showing Gandhara influence) from Devnimori (Shamlaji) in the old Idar State, now in Sabarkantha District, is to be welcomed, because it shows not only the extension of Gandhara influence in this part of India, but also the prevalence of Buddhism in Gujarat.[55] In the same

[50] Altekar, A.S., *Catalogue of the Gupta Gold Coins in Bayana*, Bombay, 1954.
[51] *Corpus of Indian Coins*, Vol. IV, Banaras, 1957.
[52] *Indian Historical Quarterly*, Vol. XVI, p. 503.
[53] Singhal, C.R., *Bibliography of Indian Coins*, Bombay, 1950.
[54] Sankalia, Deo and Ansari, *Nevasa*, p. 171.
[55] For a report with illustrations see *I.A.R.*, 1959-60, pp. 19-21, pls. XXI-XXIV.

way, the discoveries at Pitalkhora[56] of Chaitya caves and beautiful sculptures add to the existing sculptural wealth of Maharashtra. Though we have a large number of caves of the early and mediaeval periods, there were very few sculptures which could compete with such fine sculptures as the ones recently unearthed at Pitalkhora. A small inscription on the wooden rib discovered in the Chaitya cave at Bhaja again helps us in dating it to the 2nd century B.C.[57] Buddhism, it appears, was also a living force in the Madhya Pradesh, as the excavation of a Buddhist temple and Vihara at Sirpur[58] (District Raipur) shows. However, for the antiquity of Buddhism itself, the discovery of a Vihara at the famous site of Kausambi with an inscription mentioning *Ghoshitarama* (as mentioned further up) was of signal importance, because we know from Buddhist records that Buddha had gone to Kausambi and stayed in this Vihara or monastery.[59] Thus it is quite probable that the particular building was first constructed at Kausambi during the time of Buddha himself. In fact, Kausambi is such a rich site that if it is excavated fully, it will throw light on the city life in Uttar Pradesh for a number of centuries beginning with about 8th century B.C.[60] It is one of the sites which is most extensive and almost unspoiled by brick-diggers. Equally important is a stupa excavated by the late Dr. Altekar at Vaisali[61], District Muzaffarpur in Bihar. It might well be the earliest stupa built by the Lichchhavis over the relics of the Buddha.

Buddhist monasteries and Viharas have also been found at Ratnagiri[62] in Orissa. These belong to a period between 4th-5th century A D. and about 10th-11th century, showing the development of Buddhism in Eastern India, as at Nalanda and other parts in Bihar. Extensive excavations at Nagarjunakonda are of no less importance. They give us the earliest plans of a temple with a number of pillars, which afterwards became popular in South

56 *Ibid.,* 1957-58, p. 65; and *A.I.,* No. 15, 1959, pp. 66-93.

57 *I.A.R.,* 1955-56, p. 29. (Here pl. VII).

58 *I.A.R.,* 1955-56, p. 26.

59 See Sharma, G.R. in *Annual Bibliography of Indian Archaeology,* Vol. XVI, 1948-53, pl. XLI.

60 Only very recently Prof. Sharma, as mentioned above, found the palace of king Udayana.

61 *I.A.R.,* 1957-58, p. 11.

62 *Ibid.,* 1958-59, p. 33 and 1959-60, p. 38.

India. It is this place again, which has given us plans of *Yajna Kundas* (sacrificial altars), monasteries, gymnasiums, ghats and what not. In fact, as I have said before, and as I am insisting over and over again, it is only excavation of a big site which will tell us what India had achieved in the past; but for this excavation at Nagarjunakonda (carried out under the threat of impending flood) the site could never have been so extensively explored nor its rich information made available.

In the South a few more Pallava caves and structures and other temples have also been discovered.[63]

## SCULPTURE

Sculpture in India has little independent existence apart from architecture, and wherever discoveries have been reported, these have always formed part of some architectural building—a stupa or a temple. Before referring to some outstanding examples, one must note the appearance of a large number of publications— sometimes scholarly and sometimes not—on this subject. Two special journals dealing with art in general are now being regularly published—I mean *Marg* and *Lalit Kala*. There is another called *Rupalekha*. Besides there is the annual publication of the Department of Archaeology, Government of India, called *Indian Archaeology—A Review*. Almost all the new discoveries are faithfully and quickly reported. But the most admirable venture is of the Bhulabhai Memorial Institute which is trying to popularise archaeology by publishing beautifully printed small handbooks on Indian art and architecture.

If one single region has given very artistic and various types of sculptures during the last twenty years, it is south-east Rajputana and the former Idar State. Here have been found figures of gods, goddesses and others which have got a distinctive individuality and which can be compared to the classical sculpture of the Gupta period.[64] These and the later sculptures help to fill

[63] See *I.A.R.*, 1958-59, pp. 81-82.

[64] Shah, Umakant Premchand, "Sculptures from Samalaji and Roda", *Bulletin of the Baroda Museum and Picture Gallery*, Baroda 1960. See also articles by Agarwala, R.C. and others in *Lalit Kala*, Nos. 1-2, p. 130; Nos. 3-4, p. 109; No. 6, p. 63 and *Marg*, Vol. XII, p. 11.

in the gap between the Gupta and the medieval period. Even south-western Rajputana and sites like Abneri, Baroli, Ramgadh have contributed very beautiful pieces.

No less important is the huge hoard of bronzes from Akota[65], a suburb of Baroda. This again indicates that there was a school of sculpture in Western India, which could produce very varied and artistic metal images comparable to the finest from Nalanda, Nepal and Java, just before deterioration set in by too much ornamentation.

Among the early art work we must take note of the silver cup and the clay *vina* player excavated from Rupar.[66] The latter is of the 4th-5th century A.D. and is comparable in pose and technique to the one which we know from the *Vina* type coins of Samudragupta.

South India continues to yield some of its marvellous bronzes. Of these I would refer to the Nataraja[67] (now in the National Museum, New Delhi), Siva as Vrishavahana with Parvati and Vishnu with Lakshmi[68], all of the 11th century from Tiruvenkadu, Tanjore District. Noteworthy too are the still earlier Chola[69] and Pallava[70] images.

No less remarkable is a figure in stone carved in a temple in Mysore which Dr. Seshadri identifies as *Sandhya-tandava*[71] (Siva dancing a particular form ("Twilight") of his famous dance, known as *tandava*). It is much earlier than the later bronzes from South India.

Since a number of sites are being excavated all over India, we are getting every year more and more and varied—and at times very beautiful—terracottas (figures in baked clay). A time has therefore come to prepare a monograph on this subject, as the earlier works of Coomaraswamy, Gordon and Das Gupta were based on surface collections. Among the most beautiful, I would

[65] Shah Umakant P., *Akota Bronzes,* Department of Archaeology, Govt. of Bombay, 1959.

[66] *Lalit Kala,* Nos. 1-2, p. 122.

[67] *Ibid.,* p. 113, fig. 7-8.

[68] *Ibid.,* Nos. 3-4, pp. 50, 55 and 102.

[69] *Ibid.,* No. 5, p. 59 and *Marg,* Vol. I, p. 66.

[70] *Marg,* Vol. IV, No. 4, p. 28.

[71] *Artibus Asiae,* Vol. XVIII, p. 117.

cite the figures from Panna[72] and Tamluk[73] in West Bengal, Kausambi[74], Ahichhatra[75] and Rajaghat[76] in Uttar Pradesh, and Nevasa[77] in Maharashtra and Ter and Kondapur on the Andhra-Maharashtra border. The last three have produced exquisite small figures with boy-like heads in kaoline. What their exact purpose was is still unknown. One from Ter with *Srivatsa-chinha* on the breast is thought to be the child Krishna. These and other sites also made terracotta figures[78] of a Mother Goddess which seems to have been introduced in India owing to the Roman contact in the first century B.C.-A.D. The remarkable thing is that this goddess has gone to south-east Asia as far as the Celebes islands.

From Ter also have been found very delicately worked ivories.[79] Whether these belong to this site or they have been worked out in other sites like Sanchi one cannot say. But their execution is very similar to the ivory discovered from Afghanistan[80] and Italy.[81] It appears that all these have been worked by a group of similar artists, all hailing possibly from Central India.

Smaller antiquities, particularly beads, bangles, tools and weapons, and stone objects like querns, are being scientifically studied and fully described in separate sections in excavation reports. All these will be extremely useful in preparing a history of material culture in India. So also the detailed identification of grains and animal remains from excavations. Not only they tell us about the antiquity of various grains, but also about the food habits of the people in different regions at different periods and the probable time when they were acquired. Thus people

[72] *Lalit Kala,* No. 6, p. 7.

[73] *I.A.R.,* 1954-55, p. 20, pls. XXXVIII-XXXIX. (Here pl. XIIa right).

[74] Kala, Satis Chandra, *Terracotta Figurines from Kausambi,* Allahabad, 1957.

[75] *A.I.,* No. 4, 1947-48, p. 104 ff.

[76] *Journal of the U.P. Historical Society,* Vol. XIV, 1941, p. 1 ff.

[77] Sankalia, Deo, and Ansari, *From History to Pre-History at Nevasa,* p. 407, fig. 183. (Here pl. XIIa left).

[78] *Artibus Asiae,* Vol. XXIII, pp. 111-23.

[79] Barrett, Douglas, *Ter,* Bombay, 1960. (Here pl. XI).

[80] *Artibus Asiae,* Vol. XIII, 1950, p. 166-80; Vol. XV, pp. 1-5. The One from Pompeii is almost similar to the one from Ter.

[81] Ivory statuette from Pompeii described as of Lakshmi by Sir Mortimer Wheeler, *Rome Beyond the Imperial Frontiers,* p. 135, pl. XIX. This description seems to be wrong.

in the Ahmadnagar District seem to have been consuming *Bajri* and Karadi oil for the last 2,000 years. When *Bajri* was introduced in India is unknown. This is the earliest recorded use. So also Karadi. Likewise other grains—wheat, rice, lentil, gram, *mung,* peas and linseed—were familiar to people in Central India by 1000 B.C.

## GAINS TO VARIOUS RELIGIONS

The discoveries mentioned above have no doubt added to the cultural wealth of the various religions like Buddhism, Jainism and Brahmanism. But when their iconographical aspect is taken into consideration, we are able to say that Tantric Buddhism had spread to Orissa from Bihar and flourished there at least upto the 10th-11th century A.D., whereas a branch of it had also spread to Western India. This has been proved by the identification of the small bronze Buddha figures from the Sopara Stupa excavated by Dr. Bhagwanlal Indraji in the last century. These are figures of Dhyani Buddhas, which are always associated with the Tantric form of worship. Similarly, identification of certain figures in the caves at Ellora also show that Tantrism of an earlier and purer type had also penetrated this part of India.

To the Brahmanic revival, I have already referred when I was describing the *yupas* from Rajputana. This, along with the Nanaghat inscription which refers to the performance of several sacrifices by the Satavahana kings and their queen Nayanika, shows that Brahmanism of a later type flourished in Central India, Rajputana and Western India from at least the 1st century B.C. to about the 6th century A.D. It was only gradually that these sacrifices were given up, even though we do find occasional references in Rashtrakuta and Yadava inscriptions to the performance of some *Yajnas* and things like that.

## REGIONAL AND DYNASTIC STUDY OF MONUMENTS

While new discoveries are being made every year, there is a great need for a systematic study of our monuments on regional and dynastic lines. Thereby I mean that we should try to correlate the various monuments to the different dynasties which ruled in a particular region and find out if these monuments differ from each other, because the rulers were different, or because they belong to different regions. It was in this way that the work on Gujarat was begun in 1934 and published in 1941.[82] Since then a study of the whole of Maharashtra[83] has been completed by 1947 at the Deccan College, though unfortunately this work has not been published in full, so far. Recently, the Department of Archaeology, Government of India, has taken up such a detailed study and so far, I understand, the Gupta and the Pallava monuments have been studied in great detail.[84] Monographs on these with all the plans, drawings, etc. are likely to be published separately within a year or two. Currently, work is proceeding on the later temples in Central India, Saurashtra and Gujarat, whereas in the south the Chola monuments have been taken up for detailed study. When these monographs are available to the scholars, it will be possible to have a full idea of the regional and dynastic variation in our monuments and also of the picture they hold up of the various changes in our social and political life.

If I am not digressing, I would suggest that for a doctorate degree students should be encouraged to take up small, but critical studies instead of some vague subjects like "Sculpture in India between 2nd century B.C. and 2nd century A.D.". For we have got, as I have said before, a number of volumes coming out every year on this subject and already there are works of first rate importance, and so, general works do not advance our knowledge considerably.

Another aspect of epigraphical studies to which I would draw your attention is what I have been calling the 'historical and cultural geography and cultural ethnography of a region from the inscriptions'. So far we have been concentrating all our attention on the political history and sometimes on the history of religion, etc., of which one can have a glimpse from inscriptions. But

[82] Sankalia, H.D., *Archaeology of Gujarat*, Bombay, 1941.

[83] Naik, A.V., *Archaeology of the Deccan*, Ph.D. thesis Bombay University and Deccan College Library, 1947.

[84] In this connexion mention must be made of the exquisitely published work on Khajuraho by Eliky Zannas and Jeannine Auboyer (the Hague, 1960) Though every aspect of the temple is not studied in detail, this is the first work where all the monuments at Khajuraho are described.

the ordinary people and places who figure in these inscriptions were not accorded that importance which was due to them. It has been shown by a very systematic and detailed study of this type that one can throw light on the various cultural influences through which a region passed as well as the administrative and geographical units which were formed from time to time in a particular region. This can be done by identifying all the place names in a region, as far as possible and comparing them with the modern place names in the region. Thus, the work on Gujarat[85] has been published, and Maharashtra[86] and the former Madhya Pradesh (Central Provinces)[87] have also been worked out, whereas studies on Rajputana, and former U.P. are about to be completed, and that on the Pallava and Chola records have begun.

### NEED OF ARCHAEOLOGICAL PLANNING

In the course of these three lectures, we have seen how considerable progress has been made in bridging the gulf between ancient Indian history and protohistory and between protohistory and prehistory. However, we do not know how at any one site—at Nevasa for instance which has given us a fairly well-documented sequence of cultures right from the Stone Age upto the 15th century A.D.—man progressed from the state of a savage and barbarian to a civilized state of life. The main reason is that our work at Nevasa or in any other part of India is of a very limited nature. We have been excavating only in depth, but not horizontally[88] so that we do not know the plans of houses, much less of the city or of the village at each particular phase of our ex-

85 Sankalia, H.D., *Studies in the Historical and Cultural Geography and Ethnography of Gujarat,* Deccan College, Poona, 1949.

86 Mulay, Sumati, *Studies in the Historical and Cultural Geography and Ethnography of the Deccan,* Ph.D. Thesis, Deccan College and Poona University, 1955, in press now.

87 Gokhale, Shobhana, *Historical and Cultural Geography and Cultural Ethnography of Madhya Pradesh,* Ph.D. Thesis, Poona University and Deccan College Library, 1960.

88 Wheeler says (*Early India and Pakistan,* p. 148) the cultural sequences do not throw light upon the society. This can come only "when determined lateral excavations over a long period succeed the easy and quickly rewarding forays".

cavation, and therefore, when an international body like the Wenner-Gren Foundation holds a symposium to discuss how man progressed in different parts of the world and owing to what contacts and influences, we cannot give a proper reply. For instance, it has always been suggested that India lies on the periphery of world movements, that right from the Stone Age, we have been receiving one influence or culture after another and that India had no share in the origination of any of these cultures. Even as early as the First Stone Age or the Early Stone Age, it was Africa which gave us the handaxe and its developments. Later again it is quite possible that the Mesolithic cultures came to us from Africa or Western Asia and, at the dawn of civilization, it is now definitely asserted by archaeologists and anthropologists that it was Western Asia, (particularly the grassy uplands over the "Fertile Crescent") which was the cradle of civilization; that agriculture, town planning and metallurgy all arose in this region and gradually spread to India. It is because of these influences that we had first our Indus Civilization and later the Chalcolithic cultures[89] of the protohistoric period. It was once again owing to the Iranian and Greek contacts in the 5th-4th century B.C. that iron was brought to India[90] and a "second urbanization"[91] was started when the Indo-Greeks built the cities at Charsada and Taxila in the Punjab. How far these very far-reaching inferences are correct in their entirety we cannot say at present. Our present evidence, of course, points to this conclusion. But I suggest that we should not simply accept them, but should try our best to get as complete evidence as possible and show if India had no share in the origination of any of these cultures. For such a kind of result, we shall have to work on a planned and co-ordinated basis. During the last ten years, archaeology has come to the Universities. There are six Universities now in India which have full-fledged departments of archaeology and which, if they want, can carry out systematic excavations in dif-

[89] However, for other view see above, p. 98.

[90] Wheeler, Sir Mortimer, *Early India and Pakistan*, pp. 24 and 171.

[91] Sankalia, H.D., "From Food Collection to Urbanization in India" in the Symposium, "From 15,000 B.C. to the Thresholds of Urban Civilization—A world-wide Consideration of the Cultural Alternatives", July 2-11, 1960, by the Wenner-Gren Foundation for Anthropological Research at Burg Wartenstein, Austria.

ferent parts of India. The Department of Archaeology, Government of India, is also doing work on a very large scale in different parts of India, and has, since 1941, also tried to co-operate with Universities and research institutions. However, what we feel is the absence of a co-ordinated plan. These are the days of planning. And if we go on doing this work in an isolated, uncoordinated manner, then our objectives may not be achieved.

I, therefore, have been suggesting for the last few years a plan[92] in which we take into consideration the purely regional problems, then the national problems, and thirdly the international problems, because in a country like India we cannot say that this institution or that institution should not carry out excavations or exploration. We have got to provide for the varying geographical and developmental needs of a University or an institution, or a State Government department. But at the same time, we have got to create a machinery by which larger problems of national or international character can be attempted on a very, very large scale. For this we surely require a joint expedition either between two universities, as the Deccan College has been doing with the Maharaja Sayajirao University of Baroda and the State of Madhya Pradesh or between the Universities and the Government of India. A joint expedition like this can attempt to solve the Aryan problem, which I call not a national problem, but a problem in which the whole world is interested. For the solution of the Aryan problem we require a joint exploration followed by excavation by the Government of India, Universities and foreign Governments like those of Pakistan and Iran. For, as long as the area now in Pakistan and the Indo-Iranian borderland remains unexplored, we shall not be able to solve the Aryan problem by working only in India.

The second is the Neolithic problem. How did man take to agriculture, to the art of domestication of animals? From where did the polished stone implements come to India? Did they come from the East—from China and Java and Burma or from Iran

92 See Sankalia, H.D., *Archaeology and Indian Universities*, 1952, p. 5 and also Wheeler, R.E.M., "Archaeological Planning for India", *Ancient India*, No. 2, 1946, pp. 125-33, where the need of a study of physical sciences like geology, chemistry, botany is stressed.

and Central Asia. Here again no work of large-scale and of systematic nature has been done in Eastern India. In case some work is done, we shall have to carry it across through Burma to Java and Indonesia to tie up the evidence we get from India. Naturally this will require co-operation from these eastern countries.

The same is true of the Megalithic problem. We have got, as I have said in the beginning of my lecture, a Dolmen or Megalithic port-hole cist in almost all the districts of South India. Now, this is a feature of the European Megalithic monuments[93] and Wheeler has pointed out that some kind of megaliths are to be found near Karachi[94] but these have not yet been explored. Then there are megaliths in Iran. So it is possible that these can be connected, but only if explorations and excavations are undertaken with a view to examining these problems.

Problems of national importance such as the civic life in the early historical period, for instance those of the Maurya or the Gupta and the Satavahana, can only be known if such big sites like Kausambi and Hastinapur in U.P., Ujjain, and Maheshwar in M.P., Kundinapura and Paithan in Maharashtra and Kaveripattanam in South India are fully excavated. I have mentioned only a few. There are many, many more. These can be excavated horizontally provided the Universities and other institutions pool their resources in men and material and come forward with a plan. If such a plan is prepared, then as I have said, there will be room enough for small institutions not only to give training to their *alumni,* but also to carry out excavations of a purely regional character. But what we need most is a well co-ordinated plan.

[93] Childe, Gordon, "Megaliths" in *Ancient India,* No. 4, 1947, p. 1.

[94] This impression now seems to be confirmed by Fairservis whose recent survey in the district of Las Bela in South-Eastern Baluchistan has revealed a large number of stone rings, avenues, etc. *Illustrated London News,* August 26, 1961, pp. 324-27.

# INDEX

# INDEX

Instead of a simple index of names of places and persons, an attempt has been made to provide a "Cultural" index as well. And I am indebted to my colleague, Dr. S. B. Rao, for helping me in its preparation—H.D.S.

129

74; in Deccan chalcolithic, 97; invasion of, 70; problem of, 100, 125; using Painted Grey Ware, 97; traits and Indus culture, 69; tribes, 72

*Ashramas,* fourfold, 27

Asiatic Society, 2

Asoka, 110; Aramaic edict of, 110; importance of edicts of, 26, 71, 103, 109; teachings of 110, 111

Assam 72, 73, 99; and ancient Indian history, 29; and early stone age, 34; microlithic, 100; neolithic, 46

*Asvamedha* sacrifice, 112

Auboyer, Jeannine, on Khajuraho, 122 f.n. 84

Australia, stone age in, 28

Avanti, 71

Avenues (megalithic), in Baluchistan, 126 f.n. 94

Awls, 43, 92

Axes, copper, 91, 92; Navdatoli, 92; polished stone, 92

BABYLONIAN Texts, on the Geography of Western India, 69

Badari, Black-and-Red Pottery at, 78

Badopal, terracottas from, 106

Bahal 77, 88; skeletal remains at, 95

Bahrain, seals from, 68

Baigas, 96

*Bajri* (millet), 107, 121

Baked bricks, 53

Baluchistan, affinities to Painted Grey Ware, 76; and megaliths, 126 f.n. 94; pottery of Indus fabric in, 10

Banas, (River), 77, 79

Banditaccia, 20, 21

Banerjee, (Dr.), K.D., 42 f.n. 30, 102 f.n. 12

Banerjee, N.R., 101 f.n. 15

Banerji, Adris, on megaliths of Bihar, 100 f.n. 2

Bangarh, 8

Bangles, 91, 120

Bara, excavations at 53, 54; Harappan site, 51; pottery forms from, 52

Barker, 17 f.n. 8

Baroda, Akota in, 119; archaeological work in, 6

Baroda Museum, *Bulletin,* 118 f.n. 64

Baroda University, stone age work by, 34

Baroli sculptures, 119

Barrett, Douglas., on Ter 120 f.n. 79

Basin, 53

Bastar, 96

*Baudhayana Dharmasutra,* 112

Bayana, hoard of Gupta coins, 116

Beads, 91, 120, in mesolithic Gujarat, 45; of carnelian 61, 94; of copper, 94; of gold, 60; of steatite, 81; of terracotta, 81

Beaker, 59; cylindrical, 53

Bear, in terracotta, 54

Beas (River), palaeoliths from, 34 f.n. 17

Belshe, J. C., and "archaeomagnetism", 19 f.n. 9

Bengal (West), neolithic remains in, 45; stone age finds in, 34

Bengalis (Gaudiya), 115

Bhadar, (River), 63, 64

Bhagwanlal, Indraji, and epigraphy, 3; and Sopara Buddha, 121

Bhaja, Chaitya cave at, 117; inscription from, 117

*Bhakti* cult, 113

*Bhal,* (Guj.), 56, 58

Bharatput State, Bayana board from, 116

Bhatinda, (Dist.) Harappan remains in, 51

Bhillas, 96

Bhils, 96

Bhilwara, 77

Bhogavo (River), 56

Bhulabhai Memorial Institute, 118

Bhita, 5

Bhola Nath, 92 f.n. 188

Bihar, 111; aborigins in, 96; and ancient Indian history, 29; Buddhism in, 117; extent of Painted Grey Ware in, 74; megaliths in, 100; stone age finds in, 34

Bikaner, Cemetery H pottery in, 106; ceramic affinity with Cem. H, 70; ceramic peculiarities, 54; exploration in, 76 f.n. 162; explored by Stein, 72; extent of Indus culture near, 50; Painted Grey Ware in, 74; terracotta from, 106

Bikkun, Harappan site, 51

Bilingual inscription, of Asoka, 110

Birbal Sahni Institute, Lucknow, 86 f.n. 178

Birbhanpur, 46